The
Highman–de Limur
Hypotheses

The Highman–de Limur Hypotheses

by
Arthur Highman and Charles de Limur

Nelson-Hall nh Chicago

Library of Congress Cataloging in Publication Data

Highman, Arthur.
    The Highman-de Limur hypotheses.

    Includes index.
    1. Organization. 2. Management. I. De Limur,
Charles, 1923– joint author. II. Title.
HD31.H4883   658.4   79–28660
ISBN 0–88229–702–3

Copyright © 1980 by Arthur Highman and Charles de Limur

Manufactured in the United States of America

10 9 8 7 6 5 4 3 2 1

To Edith and Nonie, without whose encouragement
and enthusiasm this book would never have been written

Contents

Foreword   ix
Preface   xiii
Myths:
1. Big Business Is Run by Big Businessmen   1
2. Performance of Big Enterprise Is
    Determined by the Ability of Its Management   21
3. The Principal Objective of
    Managers, or Administrators, Is to
    Maximize an Organization's Performance   27
4. Large Enterprises Are More
    Efficient Than Small Enterprises   41
5. Organization Structures in Practice
    Conform to Commonly Stated
    "Principles" of Good Management   45
6. Delegation of Responsibility Carries
    with It Coextensively the Delegation of Authority   55
7. Organizational Lines of Authority
    and Responsibility Should Be Clear-Cut   65
8. The Amount of Autonomy
    Enjoyed by an Organizational Unit Is Determined
    by Specific and Rational Rules   73

9. The Board of Directors Controls Top Management, and Top Management Controls the Organization 77

10. The Individuals Who Manage an Organization Work for Common Goals in the Management of That Organization 85

11. Participative Management Is More Effective Than Autocratic Management (The Orange Shirt Principle) 89

12. Secure and Happy People Are More Productive Than the Insecure and the Unhappy 101

13. Managers, and Other People, Prefer Challenge to Routine 111

14. Systematic Formal Appraisals Motivate 115

15. Management by Objectives Is Basic to Good Management 123

16. Good Planning Is Based on Objective Forecasts, Analyses, and Rational Choices among Alternatives 133

17. A Budget for an Organization Is an Intellectually Logical Plan; It Curtails Waste and Unnecessary Expenditures 139

18. Overhead Is a Fixed Expense 151

19. Research and Development Is Generally a Good Investment 155

20. Ethical Conduct Takes Precedence Over Expediency 167

Index 177

Foreword

It is time, I believe, that American business schools and the doctrines which they have sought to spread throughout the land be demythologized. If they were so right at Harvard and Stanford and at all of those countless numbers of business schools in the provinces which ape their methods, how come the performance of corporate America has been so wrong lately? How come we seem to have entered a period of indefinite stagflation? How come everybody hates the oil companies and the people who run them? How come Jane Fonda is able to take on the entire energy *cum* public utility corporate establishment and win? Could it be that . . .?

It is now part of conventional wisdom that the woeful performance of the British economy is not exclusively the fault of the greedy Marxist trade unions of that country. It is recognized that the ossification of the class that owns and runs corporate Britain might be at least as much at fault. My feeling is that similar fault can today be increasingly found with the people who are running our corporations, and thus to a very great degree, our lives. Like the fellows who have been running Chrysler Corporation into the ground. Like the fellows who in-x   FOREWORD

sisted that Three Mile Island was impossible even while it was
happening. Like the fellows who were dumb enough to display
those obscene profits at the oil companies and thus divert public attention from the crucial fact that we indeed have a true
oil shortage which is a threat to our national security. If these
are the best and brightest that our business schools have been
producing during the past decades, maybe somebody out there
in B-School Land ought to be organizing an agonizing reappraisal of what they have been teaching.

Just such a reappraisal—though not agonizing, and not
couched in such critical terms—is offered to us by Arthur
Highman and Charles de Limur. When I first picked up their
manuscript I must confess that I thought, "Oh brother, another
one of these cute takeoffs on *The Peter Principle.*" Not so.
This book is very cleverly written, but not cute. It neatly sums
up business principles that differ radically from the norm and
yet does not indulge in clichés. It is well written—taut and
admirably organized. It tells us many things that we knew but
were afraid to say: that management runs boards, and not the
other way around, and that this is unhealthy for all concerned;
that Management by Objectives (MBO) is, for the most part,
nonsense, or in the words of the authors "meaningless . . . frustrating and restrictive." That "secure and happy people have
less incentive to work hard than do insecure and unhappy
ones." That "the greater the detail in a budget, the greater is
likely to be waste and unnecessary expenditure." It tells us
how to *hide,* not display, profits, a discipline in which the
Exxon management should have taken a crash course, had one
been available.

Whether you are one of the ossified class on top, or whether
you are just a simple $50,000 a year labourer well down in the
corporate hierarchy, I think you will find this book fun, en-
lightening and perhaps even valuable. More than a couple of
times I caught myself thinking: "You know, these guys are
right! Maybe I can use this."

Even if you can't use any of this book to help improve your

corporation's performance, the very fact that you will now be able to refer authoritatively to the Highman-de Limur hypotheses will probably impress the hell out of your boss and/or subordinates. And this would be quite in keeping with one of their hypotheses, namely, "Number One's priority is Number One"—and not the organization.

PAUL E. ERDMAN

Preface

This book is about managers, and about the contradiction between what is and what is supposed to be in managing. Those who run our corporations—and our schools and hospitals and government bureaus—greatly affect the lives of all of us. So do the graduate schools of business which have taught them. Have the schools and the managers done a good job?

Yes, but no. Not really good enough, for we know the nation faces serious problems, and public distrust of those who run our enterprises is rampant. What's wrong? The answer may lie partly in a reappraisal of how managers think and operate. This book represents an effort towards that reappraisal.

Twenty "myths" or commonly accepted tenets of good management are covered in twenty chapters. In discussions built around these, an attempt is made to point out how the art of managing differs from that which is commonly taught and widely accepted. The importance of the human element is considered in explaining why the usual doctrines don't always work in practice.

The summaries at the end of each chapter comprise a total of forty-five hypotheses that describe, albeit with a bit of tongue in cheek, what we believe to be realities in managing.

The book is aimed at both managers and the managed. To the knowledgeable and sophisticated in management the book should serve to define more clearly what they already know and to recall what they may have forgotten. To the novice in management and to the managed, it should serve to explain why all kinds of apparently illogical things occur in organizations and why some things don't get done that should.

The Highman-de Limur Hypotheses is intended to provoke serious thought. It raises a number of questions about common perceptions of what constitutes good management. It is hoped that in a future book these questions, and ways to better adapt the realities of management to the needs of society, can be further explored.

The extensive help of Erika Pilat in preparing the manuscript is gratefully acknowledged. Thanks are also particularly due to Charles Friedman for his delightful cartoons and to Charles de Limur, Jr., for the design of the book's dust jacket.

1
Big Business Is Run by Big Businessmen

Reality: This is a fallacy. Big business, just as truly as big government, basically is run by administrators, that is, bureaucrats.

Risk taking is at the core of the free enterprise or business system. The businessman[1] therefore can be defined as one whose function is the taking of risks, for profit. The risk taker in our economic system is the entrepreneur, and it is he, therefore, who is the true businessman. The ones who run our large businesses are managers. They are primarily administrators, not risk takers. They have to be, if organizations of any considerable size are to be run effectively.

They, the managers, occasionally do have to, or do decide to, take risks. To the extent that they do, there is some of the businessman in them. Yet their prime concern is the administration of their enterprises. This is what should be expected, particularly with large organizations, and especially in mature industries.

There are decided differences between the true businessman,

---

1. For smoothness and simplicity, the male form will be used throughout the text.

the entrepreneur, and most managers, in both personal characteristics and outlook.

The entrepreneur is a gambler. He is able to see a business opportunity and is willing to seize it, to work, struggle, and persist with it and its accompanying risks, to build a business where none existed before. He tends to be a driven man with a fierce desire for independence, impatient of the necessary restraints imposed in the functioning of a large organization.

The manager, an administrator, tends to be a coordinator, someone who will manage the routine and details of running an ongoing enterprise that is already well established. The manager has a touch of the conservator in him: he conserves existing assets and maintains the status quo, albeit with an eye to growth—sometimes modest, at other times relatively dynamic. He is not fundamentally a risk taker, a gambler. If the manager-administrator does take risks, it is likely to be when he cannot avoid them—or when the very nature of the circumstances, or the business engaged in, requires him to choose among alternative risks, including that of doing nothing, which may be the biggest risk of all. The manager's actions tend to be governed by a desire to minimize risk, for the firm and so also for himself, rather than to maximize profits, for the stockholder.

To a degree, the businessman-entrepreneur can be likened to the individual who is inclined to gamble his paycheck at the racetrack, for the potential of a large gain. The manager, on the other hand, may be likened to the one who on payday conservatively takes his check home to pay his bills and if possible to retain some of it for only a modest addition to his net assets.

The type of individual who makes a good entrepreneur tends not to make a good manager, and the reverse. Some individuals are outstanding as both entrepreneurs and managers, but not many. Henry Ford and John D. Rockefeller in the past filled both roles, though admittedly their autocratic management styles might not play so well today. David Packard of Hewlett-

Manager or a businessman-entrepreneur?

Packard and possibly rock impresario Bill Graham could be cited as examples today of those able to play the combined role.

Among those who control large enterprises, a few are financiers or "wheeler-dealers." If these develop new businesses rather than merely merge or spin off and recombine already existing businesses, they are true entrepreneurs. In the large enterprise, however, even where a wheeler-dealer, or occasionally a founding entrepreneur, controls, the actual daily running of the ongoing business is likely to be in the hands of a manager, an administrator.

The entrepreneur is important in the founding of a business, when a business is small and the risk great. When a firm becomes larger and established, risk and the need for risk taking are less. It's then that a company needs an administrator, a good manager whose prime objective is to administer. The manager is not generally an owner of the large enterprise to any but a minor degree. This is a fact that adds to a natural aversion to risk taking. The manager's potential personal rewards as a nonowner for taking risks and succeeding don't match the personal penalties—loss of bonus, demotion, even discharge—for taking risks and failing. There is little personal gain generally from performance much beyond that which is expected—that holding in the recent past plus modest progression.[2]

In taking over small, successful, and growing companies, a large organization is likely to find that eventually the entrepreneur-founder has to be replaced with someone who is primarily an able manager. Both continued growth in size and the constraints of operating within the framework of a large enterprise make the ability to manage essential, and more valuable than the ability to initiate, innovate, and take risks. If a founder is not sufficiently competent as a manager, if he does not have enough of the touch of the bureaucrat, politician, and team player, he cannot function effectively in his altered role.

Let's consider that further. Suppose an entrepreneur-founder starting a business happens also to be a good manager. He will undoubtedly play a leading role as a manager and continue to be involved with the business as it grows. However, if the entrepreneur is not a good manager, one of two alternatives is likely to occur. In the first place, he could hire a manager to run the business while retaining a position on the board of directors. Alternatively, if he does not recognize his managerial limitations, he will end up either by leaving the firm he founded— if it doesn't go bankrupt first—or being pushed out by other parties who are financially interested in the company. In this situation he has reached his "level of incompetence" (see *The*

---

2. See chapter 3.

Peter Principle by Laurence J. Peter and Raymond Hull), and
the shareholders have reached the end of their patience.
With increasing size there will be an increasing load of details and administrative problems to tie up the entrepreneur.
Even one who is a good manager may find the fun in running
the business is no longer there. The founder can then decide
to sell out for a capital gain and retire. If he doesn't want retirement, or tires of it later, he may exercise his gambling in-
stincts again and found a new enterprise. This has happened
time and again in the electronics industry: a founder-entre-
preneur has discovered after a few months, or a year or two,
that simply being a millionaire, with time on his hands, is not
enough. The new millionaire becomes an entrepreneur again,
and a new venture is born.

As the company grows, the need for additional capital brings
in outside stockholders—private venture capitalists, or on
occasion the investing public at large—and insurance companies or banks as sources of loans. If initial growth continues,
still more capital is needed, and a situation develops where part
of the price of that capital comes to be loss of control. The
founder no longer owns the majority of the stock, even if
originally he did.

As the company grows further, problems of management
become paramount. And here again, if the founder is qualified
as a manager, growth and increases in profits will continue
under his direction. On the other hand, if he has no managerial
qualifications, growth will suffer, and profits will not come up
to expectations. In fact, losses may even occur. It is then that
the investors or those who represent them—in some cases the
investment bankers or even the commercial banks or other
lenders—exert the necessary pressure to replace the entrepreneur with someone who can manage.

It is not unusual to see the bitter founder who complains
that he has been pushed out of his own business by politics, the
disloyalty of ambitious subordinates, or the ignorance and
greed of investors and lenders. He overlooks his own man-

agerial shortcoming—though sometimes it is true that the
founder is pushed out for reasons other than managerial inadequacy. There may be disagreements with investors over
goals, policies, and expansion. Occasionally, in truth, personalities and politics play a part. An undue diversion of time to
noncompany activity, or health, and a number of additional
reasons also may be involved.

We can formulate an hypothesis: *Entrepreneurial risk taking is inversely proportional to the size of a firm.* (This hypothesis holds for similar risk taking for nonprofit entities as
well.) As a firm grows larger there is decreasing need, and
perhaps lessening opportunity, for entrepreneurship. Moreover, the costs of failure become larger, and this too discourages entrepreneurial risk taking.

Synergism stemming from established position can almost
carry the larger firm and allow it to continue growing, without
the necessity for more than a minimum of risk taking. By
synergism, we mean here the effect of established customers
and distribution channels; friendships, tie-ins, and reciprocity;
the inertia of customers who grow but stay with the same
supplier; brand loyalties; the weight of continuous advertising
and sales calls; patents; government regulators whose actions
often favor the established and larger firms, and other business
interrelationships all acting together.

The assumption that entrepreneurial risk taking decreases
with size might at first glance be questioned by citing examples
of considerable risk taking by large firms, particularly by firms
in mining, oil exploration, and high technology. In these areas,
however, the very nature of the industries concerned makes
failure to take risks of itself perhaps the riskiest of all the
decisions a manager can make. Large firms in those industries
sometimes take considerable risks because taking those risks
is a necessity. It is part of the business. Yet even in those industries, the smaller firms are the most entrepreneurial. Relative to size, they are still the ones who take the biggest gambles.

Even if a nonowner manager is willing to take risks, a perceived need for his own survival—or the retention of his present position, satisfactions, and future prospects—will discourage him from taking more risks than are necessary to achieve the level of performance expected of him. Let's illustrate.

Assume that a return of 12 percent on invested capital is all that is expected by a company's stockholders and board of directors. This is rated good performance. If this can be accomplished with relative safety, why should a manager gamble on risky investments or actions that can bring a 25-percent return, but with the chance of losing a bonus or a promotion, being demoted, or even being fired if he fails? If he succeeds and makes the 25 percent, will he only raise expectations and lock himself into having to do it again next year? Are the possible rewards worth the risks?

Look at it another way. Suppose a large organization has an opportunity to invest $1 million in each of twenty projects. Each has a 30-percent chance of failure, with the loss in that case of the $1 million, but no more. If successful, each will yield a return of 40 percent annually on the capital invested. The twenty projects, overall, will yield a return of 28 percent (70 percent chance of success times 40 percent return if successful).

Alternatively, assume the organization can invest $1 million in each of twenty other projects. Each has only a 5-percent chance of failure, but each if successful will yield a return of only 20 percent annually on the capital. The alternate twenty projects will yield an overall return of 19 percent (95-percent chance of success times 20-percent return if successful).

Assume the expected average return for the company overall is 15 percent on investment, with an actual attainment historically of only 12 percent.

Now assume the selection of two of the twenty projects is separately the responsibility of each of ten managers. How many of those ten managers will voluntarily choose or dream up and push for, two projects, or even one project, carrying a return of 40 percent, but with a 30-percent risk of failure? Is it indeed likely that most, probably all, will be satisfied with projects yielding a 20-percent return and only carrying a 5-percent chance of failure? After all, how many failures will a manager be forgiven? Even a 20-percent return is good performance when only 12 percent has been achieved in the past and but 15 percent is currently expected.

Two successful projects each carrying a 20-percent return on investment likely will get a manager just as great a promotion, and as quickly, as will two successful projects each carrying a 40-percent return on investment. Moreover, a manager opting for risky 40-percent projects, even if he is lucky and succeeds with both, may be in danger of being tagged as too prone to gamble on questionable projects. And if the "gamble-prone" manager fails with even one of his two projects, well then . . .??

Enough of the figures. What we are really saying is that higher-risk investments, carrying a greater return, may be best for the organization, but they certainly are not best for the individual manager. From a theoretical standpoint, in a decision involving risk a manager will choose the alternative that maximizes his net "utility." The "disutility" of the greater failure potential, 30 percent as against a 5-percent failure risk in the example above, is greater than the "utility" of greater success potential, rewards for 40 percent compared with those for 20 percent return on investment. The penalty for risk taking and subsequent failure is much greater for the individual than for the firm. The firm can average in a few failures with successes over a period of time and in many projects. The individual is less able to do so.

It should be pointed out, however, that there are times when the perceived need for survival may increase a manager's willingness to take risks. Thus a new manager may be under heavy pressure to improve on his predecessor's poor profit performance. Failure to improve will mean being fired. The manager may perceive that considerable risk taking, with the stockholders' money, not his own, will provide survival for himself if successful. It also will provide him personal satisfactions. If considerable risks are not taken, then the likelihood of being fired will be greater. Without considerable gambling, the profit improvement will be insufficient. By maximizing the company's risk, the manager minimizes his own personal insecurity. Some corollaries of risk taking or its avoidance may be of interest. Let's discuss a few here.

Innovation of any type is a form of risk taking. New ideas, procedures, or products that depart from the existing—in manufacturing, in marketing, or otherwise—are a form of innovation. The more radical the innovation, the greater is likely to be the risk involved. To the extent that an organization reaches a point where administrative rather than entrepreneurial thinking predominates, where risk avoidance carries great weight, the tendency to be innovative becomes muted. In terms of a general tendency, other things being equal, one could argue that *the willingness to innovate varies inversely with the size of an organization.*

Administrators and managers are reluctant to encourage innovation because of personal risk. In a study for the National Science Foundation, "Barriers to Innovation in Industry," the high individual risk of being blamed for failure was among the nine barrier factors identified as most severe.[3]

Though both involve risk taking, entrepreneurship should not be confused with innovation. The latter is doing something new or making changes in or to something already existing. Entrepreneurship may or may not involve innovation.

Innovation entails risk insofar as something new may be impractical, but it is also risky if the new works and is effective. Timing is critical. For example, the Chrysler and De Soto

---

3. A. D. Little and Industrial Research Institute Report to National Science Foundation, "Barriers to Innovation in Industry—Opportunities for Public Policy Changes." (NSF–C748 and C725) Aug. 1973; as referred to by Donald M. Collier in "Research-Based Venture Companies—The Link between Market and Technology," *Research Management,* May 1974, pp. 16–20.

Administrators and managers are reluctant to encourage innovation.

"Airflow" designs of the thirties, as well as the Raymond Loewy Studebaker automobile of the forties, were both premature, being publicly unacceptable—although even by today's visual standards they probably would have failed. Innovating too soon can be as unprofitable as being too late.

Another hazard lies in the need for adequate market distribution. An innovative product has to be sold. If the competition effectively controls the channels of distribution, a new product is not likely to be successful. The same is true where competition does not control, but where the innovator doesn't have adequate distribution outlets himself. The history of companies without appropriate dealership organizations in the auto industry is legendary and illustrates this.

Volkswagen of Germany struggled in this country for years because consumers feared lack of service and repairability. After building up a large dealership organization, Volkswagen led imported car sales in the United States for years. Japanese automakers seeking U.S. sales built a dealership organization in prime markets almost as soon as new markets were penetrated. Success in opening new markets and beating the Volkswagen competition came quickly.

Besides having channels of distribution, the innovator must have marketing know-how and adequate financing. According to an article entitled "The Breakdown of U.S. Innovation," Proctor and Gamble spent some $70 million bringing Pringle's New Fangled Potato Chips, hardly a major innovation, to market.[4]

A third risk in innovation lies in its effect on present investments. Unnecessary innovation by an organization can make a company's existing investment obsolete or, at best, reduce its profitability. Naturally, in this situation the effect on existing investment does get consideration. Where money is invested in original equipment that is still good and efficient, an innovation can cause the company to add an expense before it is necessary. The push-button telephone was developed while countless numbers of dial phones were still perfectly useful. That's why it has taken time to replace the old equipment with the new push-button style.

Within an organization, successful innovation can pose risks. It can directly or indirectly threaten those members of management and the internal bureaucracy who were skeptical or opposed to the innovation, those who weren't bright enough to think of it themselves, and of course such segments of the organization as may be adversely affected by competition from the new. As we have stressed before, large businesses are run by managers and administrators. These people must make an

4. "The Breakdown of U.S. Innovation," *Business Week,* February 16, 1976, pp. 56–68.

expected level of profit and avoid as much risk as possible. When a manager is presented with a situation where he must decide to either make a satisfactory profit now or gamble on making even a much larger profit somewhere down the road, odds are that he will decide to go for the short-term profit. Let's have a closer look at this.

The administrator allocates financial resources by discounted cash-flow analyses that favor a near-term incremental increase over anticipated returns slated to materialize several years hence. To illustrate: Discounting the future at 8 percent, we calculate the amount needed now, the so-called present value, which saved or otherwise invested "now" until "then," earning 8 percent per year between "now" and "then," when withdrawn will yield the "then" value. Thus $108.00 received, say for services, at the end of one year is equal to only $100.00 now, because $100.00 invested now will earn 8 percent or $8.00 in a year. $100.00 received at the end of a year, "then," is worth only $92.60 "now" ($92.60 invested "now" for the year between "now" and "then" yields $92.60 + $7.40 interest @ 8 percent, or $100.00 a year later). Similarly, $100.00 received ten years from now and discounted at 8 percent (by the discounted cash-flow method) is today worth only $46.30. Discounted at 10 percent it is worth $38.60, at 15 percent it is worth $27.40, at 20 percent only $16.20. This is irrespective of any deflation of the dollar itself.

The pacemaker took thirty-two years to develop. You'd have to look a long way to find a manager who'd commit funds to the development of such a product today. By the discounted cash-flow method, a $1 million profit discounted at 20 percent for say only fifteen years would be equivalent to just $65,000 today.

With turnover being what it is in upper management these days, the likelihood of a manager's still being around when one of these innovations starts making a profit is anything but assured. Even the video recorder—it took only six years to develop—would be a radical risk for a manager to assume.

The engineering department isn't very different. Charged with developing designs that work reliably and safely in a cost-effective framework, engineering, like administration, is unwilling to risk reputation and jobs on new products that have not been exhaustively tested in the field.

New products and processes are costly. They require new facilities, equipment, technology, to say nothing of the cost of training the labor force to operate new machines or master new processes. Chances are the unions will resist, for it might mean loss of jobs for members and possibly loss of power for union leaders. The sales force will probably be resistant too. They have to devote time to learning about the new product and have to take more time on sales calls to educate their customers. This means that, at least initially, they have to spend more time to sell the same amount of product.

The general manager worries about all these things. He has to make a respectable profit. Why should he stick his neck out when it may detract from this year's return on investment—especially since there's a good chance the profit may not even be realized during his tenure. Why should he choose to endure the headaches of union hassles, the watchdog tactics of "everyone's favorite uncle," a resistant sales force, the necessity of new marketing strategy, and disgruntled stockholders? Small wonder that most innovations have come from outside an industry: from entrepreneurs, not managers; from small companies, not large; and often from dreamers and lunatics—at least as judged by good management criteria.

More than half of the major innovations of the twentieth century have come from small companies or independent inventors. In the decade between 1945 and 1955, the figure was two-thirds. Major innovations in an industry are not always the products of that industry. Transistors were first marketed by Texas Instruments rather than by RCA or General Electric, which were the large producers of vacuum tubes. Haloid, now Xerox, pioneered electrostatic copying—not Addressograph or Eastman Kodak, which were important in the copying field.

Polaroid and not Eastman Kodak developed instant pictures; and nylon was a product of DuPont, not of the silk industry. Of the major innovations in the steel industry, four came from Europe, seven from independent inventors, and none from the American steel industry.[5]

The desire to avoid risk, ever implicit in "good management," is well expressed in the "prudent man" rule which applies to a fiduciary in the investment of funds entrusted to its care. That rule calls for the trustee of such funds, that is, their manager, to invest in securities that others invest in—the popular, the blue chips, the fashionable securities—the ones everyone believes to be prudent investments. The trustee follows the lead of others. He conforms to the crowd. Those securities that the leaders among the managers of trust funds particularly favor become the special targets for investment by the crowd. The trustee avoids the less-popular securities. If he makes an investment mistake, it is far better to do so in good company, in which case he can be forgiven, than to do so all on his own. How many errors in judgment can he survive if those errors are in investments that are not popular, that he alone has made?

A trustee thereby discriminates against smaller firms. Smaller firms individually represent only limited amounts of capital and can provide a place to invest only a limited number of dollars. They cannot therefore be popular investments for the crowd. They represent too few dollars. Almost by definition, then, investment in smaller firms violates the prudent man rule. Trustees are decidedly discouraged by this rule from investing in smaller firms, as well as from generally showing individuality in investment decisions.

And at least in part, the same considerations spill over into investment advice. After all, relatively, how often does a smaller company's name appear on an investment advisor's list of recommendations? How often is an investor's query of his

5. See chapter 19, footnotes 13 and 14.

advisor as to a smaller firm answered with the comment, "Oh, no! We don't follow that company."

Does the prudent man rule encourage a lot of capital to pursue a limited number of eligible securities? Do returns for trustee investment therefore tend to be less than they would otherwise be, because of the concentration on and heavy demand for favored securities that are considered safely to conform to the prudent man rule? Does the prudent man rule thus help to ensure a low return for the "widows and orphans" whom the prudent man rule is supposed to protect? Interesting questions!

Perhaps we can sum up with the following: *The prudent man rule encourages conformity. It discourages initiative, innovation, and a large return on investment.*

The prudent man trustee follows the crowd, and the crowd follows its leaders. So also with business forecasting. Better for an economist, as for a prudent trustee, to be wrong in good company in forecasting than to turn out to be wrong when good company fortuitously is right. The rewards if the forecaster turns out to be right when good company is wrong just aren't enough to be worth the risks if the opposite turns out to be the case. The rewards won't be much, while punishment can be severe—no raise, or demotion, or even dismissal; survival is virtually at stake, at least with the current employer. (Of course, there always are a few mavericks or entrepreneurial-type thinkers who will stray from the crowd anyway.)

So also it goes for the senior manager who heads a manufacturing organization. He may be better off to be wrong in the good company of the majority of his colleagues in making a decision not to manufacture a new product. If he goes ahead and it turns out to be a mistake, the fault is all his. If *not* manufacturing is the wrong decision—say the competition gets the jump—he won't get all the blame because everyone concurred.

Consider further how often one runs into follow-the-leader variations of the following.

If that's what Famous predicts, and if Seconder agrees—well, then, I think so too.

Even our TV advertising suggests this follow-the-leader syndrome—for example, "When E. F. Hutton talks, people listen."

A leading executive in the petrochemical field, when asked for a forecast of the market for a new family of synthetics, simply quoted another leading expert's estimate. With the two industry leaders forecasting the identical quantity, who would have the temerity to forecast anything different? Even though the figure might have been derived quite unscientifically, who would risk his reputation by suggesting that a different estimate might be more accurate?

To illustrate other aspects of the avoidance of risk taking, there is the imaginary unspoken conversation between a doctor and his patient that shows the potential difficulties posed by both malpractice suits and governmental regulatory agencies—a "Catch 22" if you will.

We'd better stick to the tried-and-true treatment for your cancer. It has a 10-percent chance of success at this stage of your illness. We could try a new drug, but it's risky. It succeeds in 50 percent of the cases, but there is a 50-percent chance it will kill you if you take it too long.

How long?

Oh, say six months.

How much time do I live without it, if the 10-percent chance treatment fails?

Three to four months.

Well, then give me the new drug.

I can't. If I do and it doesn't work, no matter when you die, your heirs will hit me with a malpractice suit for trying a dangerous drug, particularly one that hasn't been approved yet for use in this country, by the FDA. At the very least, my insurance rates will go up.

Another form of the prudent man rule is *the principle of controlled aggressiveness* likely to hold in an organization, and in an industry. Don't grab for an increased share of the market (or, within an organization, position and authority) too fast, especially if the competition has clout and can fight back. Creep up!

That's the way two major companies in a segment of the building materials industry in the San Francisco Bay Area became three major companies. A smaller company crept up and, aided by the complacency of the two major ones, finally became the third major factor. Had it grabbed too fast, the threat would have been sharply obvious. It would not have been ignored. The two established firms could have temporarily destabilized prices or otherwise acted to prevent the gradual encroachment that allowed the third company to grow and prosper.

Similarly, some years ago, one of the two principal producers of a branded canned grocery product, Number Two, which had been creeping up on Number One gradually over a period of years, overnight vastly increased its advertising budget in the hope of grabbing off quickly a larger share of the market that the two firms shared. A quantum jump in Number Two's share of the market would have given the upstart family that controlled the firm a great deal of personal satisfaction. It didn't take long before the old-line family that controlled Number One retaliated with its own increased advertising. After both companies in less than a year had spent most of three years' profits on excessive advertising that did not permanently increase the total market or permanently affect either's share of the market, the lesson of controlled aggressiveness sank in. Advertising receded to what had been normal.

Don't rock the boat! Don't deviate too widely from the norm. It's all right to be productive and aggressive, to rise in the hierarchy, but don't forget there is danger in too far outshining others, in making others look bad. The ambitious man who far outproduces his fellow workers on the production line, and thus threatens the continuation of the established work standard, the security of the existing work pace, is not ap-

preciated. Nor does the eager beaver among white collar workers, or for that matter among middle managers or among executives, who too obviously outproduces his colleagues receive
from them, or always from his boss, an enthusiastic accolade.

One is reminded of the apocryphal remark made by a corporate vice-president of sales to the man who followed him as
sales manager of the Dallas region. He didn't particularly like
being shown up by his successor in the territory he had previously managed. The successor's boast of performance did
imply that the boss, his predecessor in the region, had not been
a particularly great performer.

> "So you've doubled sales volume in Dallas since I had the
> territory myself a year ago. Really? Mm...m. You're fired!"

To sum up, big business is not run by businessmen. Entrepreneurs are the true businessmen. They are the risk takers in
a free-enterprise system where risk taking is supposed to be
basic to the system. Big business is run by its managers, who
are primarily administrators, or bureaucrats if you will. They
tend to be conservators, not risk takers.

It should be expected that administration and, particularly
in the larger companies and mature industries, the avoidance
of undue risk are the prime objectives of managers. To a
degree this has to be so. The avoidance of risk implies, however, the discouragement of innovation, discrimination against
investment in smaller businesses, me too–ism, and generally
conformity to the norm, in our less-than-free enterprise system.

How much of our current status vis-à-vis the other economic
powers—for instance Japan and Germany—is due to this
type of management philosophy and practice is a question the
individual reader may wish to ask himself.

Hypotheses:

We may sum up this chapter with the following hypotheses:
*Entrepreneurial risk taking is inversely proportional to the
size of an organization.*

*The willingness to innovate varies inversely with the size of
an organization.*

The prudent man rule encourages conformity. It discourages initiative, innovation, and a large return on investment.

The principle of controlled aggressiveness is likely to hold in an organization, and in an industry: Creep up, don't grab!

2

Performance of Big Enterprise Is Determined by the Ability of Its Management

Reality: The achievements of large, mature organizations are more likely to be determined by the strength of their competition, and by economic, political, and other factors, than they are solely by the ability of management. *Circumstance, not management, produces results. Management is largely limited in its ability to influence performance, profits in business, so long as it is reasonably competent.* In other words, the role management plays is indeed that of the conservator-administrator —that is, in a sense the role of a caretaker.

The importance of circumstances is illustrated by the following story, somewhat disguised, but basically true, related by a management consultant.

> About three years ago I met a relatively young fellow in the high-fashion women's wear business. As head of a chain of stores he had asked me to meet him to discuss a survey he wanted done. The chain this fellow managed was a subsidiary of a multibillion-dollar retailing complex. He had taken command of the chain two years earlier, and during those two years he had achieved a remarkable turnaround, from a lackluster and generally poor performance to an outstanding one.

Profits for the chain were the best they had ever been, and this young man, a whiz kid if you will, was named executive of the year by the parent firm. He received a most generous pay increase and a bonus. Subsequently he was promoted to senior vice-president, and his duties expanded to include responsibility for an additional three subsidiaries of the parent firm. Rumor had it that he would eventually succeed the parent firm's chief executive when the latter retired.

I must say not much happened in respect to the survey work we had talked about. I did not see him again until recently, at a cocktail party. The young man was no longer connected with the women's apparel business. He was in fact currently unemployed. He had been let go six months before, and getting relocated, in a good spot, was proving to be tough.

What had happened? Very simple! The business he headed had gone downhill fast, starting almost as soon as he had been made senior vice-president. After two of the best years ever, sales of the chain of high-fashion stores turned down drastically. Financial results for the last year of his executive tenure were among the worst the chain had ever had, and the other three subsidiaries under his wing had not done well either. The blame had to be pinned somewhere, and this young fellow was the logical man for it.

Yet he was the same man with the same abilities—when the years had been good and when they went sour. Of course, there was a difference. The good years had been good for the rest of the fashion industry too. The bad years had been bad for everybody. The economic situation, trends in fashion, a switch in women's buying habits—a lot of factors other than merchandising talent and management ability were at work.

Yes, indeed! Yesterday's whiz-kid manager does sometimes turn into today's misfit. The difference between the brilliant professional and the stupid amateur among executives, as between the shrewd businessman and the bum, often is circumstance—luck if you will. Of course, even if circumstances are right, it helps to have a reasonable amount of ability. This is illustrated by a dialog overheard at a seminar, after a discussion of published financial statements—

The old (yesterday's whiz kid, today's misfit) goes out!
The new "genius" arrives.

Have you ever noticed? When one cement company has a
good year, so do the others. When one supermarket chain has
a bad year so do its competitors. This doesn't prevent management from congratulating itself, of course, in statements to its
stockholders, when years are good—something like, "By dint
of its ability your management has raised profits this year by
fully 25 percent." Of course, economic conditions may have
helped, a little bit, and the competitors also may have increased their profits, maybe by more than 25 percent.

Yes, and when the economy adversely affects earnings,
management makes damn sure the economy gets its full share
of the blame.

Just how much does performance, profits of a firm, or occu-
pancy rates in a hospital, depend on the business cycle and

other factors, and how much does it depend on the ability of the managers—at least on ability beyond that necessary to bring them to their elevated managerial positions? The question is legitimate. Some managers get extremely good pay for their talents, and the real worth of those talents relative to the pay received indeed can be questioned. This is so at least for large enterprises in mature industries. Is it realistic to believe that an executive who receives a total annual compensation in the $750,000 to $1 million–plus range (there are a few who do) can, by the very uniqueness of his own special talents, truly have much effect on the destiny of his company? We really don't believe so.

"By dint of its ability your management has raised profits this year by fully 25 percent."

A review of profits for a large number of English companies by Oxford professor I. M. D. Little, and an American study of data on changes in profits in the United States for 700 industrial firms between 1945 and 1964, reveal a "random walk" pattern of profits. Future profit-growth rates cannot be predicted from the past.[1] Yet if management ability were the major determinant of past and future profits, one would expect some considerable correlation between past and future rates of growth in earnings. The random walk pattern does not prove, but does imply, that the abilities of managers, the heads of corporations, in most cases have less to do with determining profit levels than do circumstances. Nevertheless, despite the doubts, it may still well behoove a firm to compete with whatever salary and other incentives are required for what in its opinion is the best management talent it can get. For a large firm, even a small increase in profit traceable to management ability can more than pay for some very large financial rewards to its key managers.

Of course, as with so many things, how does one go about evaluating talent, or the lack of it?

Hypothesis:

Summing up, we may postulate that *circumstance, not management, produces results. Management is largely limited in its ability to influence performance, profits in business, so long as it is at least reasonably competent.*

---

1. See *Barron's,* February 28, 1977, p. 21.

3

The Principal Objective of Managers, or Administrators, Is to Maximize an Organization's Performance

Reality: The principal objective of managers, or administrators, is the assurance first of their own survival. *Number One's priority is Number One.* Assuming no concern about its own survival, the primary goals of management include the maximization of personal satisfactions, whatever these may be; then survival, and progress however defined, for the organization. It is only after these that maximizing performance for the organization ranks as a concern.

Of course the priorities intermesh. The situation is a little like the chicken and the egg. Survival, progress, and performance for the organization are important to management's own survival, and to its satisfactions. Yet optimal managerial achievements for the organization are predicated upon management's survival and the fulfillment of management's personal goals.

Not long ago the president of a firm faced a difficult situation. It was projected that profits for the year coming to a close would be 50 percent ahead of those for the previous year. This would never do. The president felt he had to bring profits down to a more modest but still respectable figure.

Otherwise he would have a real problem, for he doubted the
following year's profits could be sustained at such a high
level. Yet his board of directors would expect greater profits
than in the current year. After all, shouldn't each year be a
little bit better than the preceding one?

So, what did the president do? He determined that, if profits for the year just finishing up were cut to 20 percent over
the preceding year, he could certainly show a further 20-per-
cent increase in the following year. In this manner he would
keep his board happy. He could cut profits, whether real or
apparent, in a number of ways, some of which are described
later in this chapter. He did exactly that, and both he and his
board were happy.

The president did not think in terms of maximizing results.
He was really more concerned about what might be good for
himself. (This could be rationalized into terms of what was
good in the long run for the enterprise. With some justification, perhaps, the continuity of management was part of
what was good for the enterprise.) This is to be expected. Yet
a common assumption in the literature of management and
economics has been the myth that managements, those who
run our business enterprises, operate to maximize profits; or
in the nonprofit segment of the economy managements act to
maximize performance, however that be measured. The assumption is simply not true.

What is true for a company's president is true also for his
subordinates. Thus pursuing further the example of a president
faced with a sudden increase in profit, let us assume profits
of a company division could be doubled in one year. How
many division managers would show such a doubling, if it
had not been customary to double each year? Surely, doubling
means raising expectations, and wouldn't this make it difficult
for the manager for the following year? Might a sudden doubling of profits in one year even encourage questions as to why
profits were only half as much before? Maybe they should have
been higher before, and maybe they should not have. But

whichever way one looks at it, sudden doubling could be bad for the manager's "professional health."

Let's look at the same situation in a different form. There are many department managers who likely could improve their operations sufficiently to cut expenses by, say, 20 percent in one year. If they could do so, would they? In other words, if one is expected to cut expenses by 5 percent, would one actually cut by 20 percent if this could be done, or would he cut by 7 percent or maybe 8 percent? The latter does show a respectably better performance than expected, and yet it provides room for further cutting if a manager should be asked to do so in the next year.

Will a public utility manager voluntarily operate close to the bone, thus taking a chance of real financial problems with rising costs? Suppose a requested rate increase is delayed by the public utility commission or halved or both? If the utility manager operates with a certain amount of "fat" that can be trimmed if rate increases granted are delayed or lower than requested, does he thus avoid difficult financial problems? Can he really be expected continually to maximize performance, that is, to operate lean? Will he?

That a manager's personal objectives, starting with survival, do have some priority over those for the organization can be easily demonstrated. For instance, how often will the president of a firm volunteer to resign to make way for a subordinate who he believes can produce greater profits for the firm? Or does a president always believe that no one else in his organization, or from the outside, can produce more than he can? Or how often will a department head voluntarily resign in favor of a more capable assistant? And how often, in the nonprofit area, will a hospital administrator remove himself and recommend a successor who, he feels, can outperform him in improving patient care and cutting costs?

One should pause here to note that, although personal survival is a manager's first-priority objective, survival in a manager's view need not necessarily be with his current organi-

"I like my job, but I'm resigning. He can make more money
for you. Maximizing profit—that's what's important!"

zation. If a manager believes he can survive severance, he may
deliberately leave his present employer and move to another
in order to better attain goals other than his survival—namely,
personal satisfactions. These may include opportunities for
greater personal performance with another firm.

The attainment of personal satisfactions is important to a
manager, once survival is not a concern. Satisfactions are likely
to include a sense of accomplishment. They also include
money, power, status, and prestige, not to mention a desire
to live in or near a particular city.[1] For example, Phoenix,
Arizona, surely is not the transportation center of the United

---

1. "When Business Moves Where the Boss Lives," *Business Week*,
   September 30, 1972, p. 69.

States. Then why did the chief executive of Greyhound Corporation move the corporate headquarters to that city from Chicago? A similar question could be addressed to other, though certainly not all, corporate moves. Personal satisfactions for management don't always coincide with the needs of the organizations managed.

Survival and personal satisfaction are, however, linked with performance. In business enterprises, this generally means profits. A common criterion is profit per dollar invested. *Dollars invested* may refer to total capital employed or only to stockholders' capital. The latter excludes borrowed funds. How capital investment is defined can make a considerable difference in measuring performance. *Performance* has many different meanings. For the manager of a manufacturing department, it may refer to the cost per unit of output. For the head of a sales division, it may mean sales volume achieved or the sales department's contribution to overhead and profit. To a manager of a college placement bureau, it may mean the number of graduates placed in meaningful positions. And for universities, it may mean growth in buildings, faculty, courses, and students.

As to the last, it may be of interest to note that, to obtain growth for a private university, it may very well be necessary to operate at a loss—in other words, to aim for a "nonperformance" from a strictly profit standpoint. It has been widely surmised that alumni can be marshalled more easily to contribute to the rescue of their alma mater from the crisis of a budget deficit—albeit brought on by enlarging operations and promoting growth before and not after the money for this is available—than to donate money to a university that is operating in the black.

Capable college presidents presumably are aware of this principle. So, for that matter, are those in charge of opera companies, museums, and other nonprofit activities. Public school administrators and others, too, have been aware that, at least in the past, taxes could be raised more readily when

*"The University is in the black. We simply can't afford that
if we want the alumni to contribute."*

a fiscal crisis threatened the local public school district than
when budgets were balanced. It is quite possible that the now
famous Proposition 13 of California might not have received
such overwhelming voter approval had the state not had a
whopping budget surplus.

Performance means many different things to different
people, but in business it really has only one connotation—
profits. Stockholders, boards of directors, and the banks who
have loaned money they want repaid establish certain expectations of performance, that is, profits. These expectations
are directly relevant to a manager's goals.

It is true that, contrary to the usual diagrammatical organization of a corporation, stockholders and the board commonly

do not control a company and its management. Rather, management ordinarily controls its board, and the stockholders really have little to say about either who constitutes the board or how the company is run. Nevertheless, stockholder and board expectations do play a role. They are relevant.

If performance is really poor compared to that which a board or the stockholders expect, and if it continues so for some time, then either or both may revolt and exercise the control over management that legally they do have, much to the discomfort of management.

And so once again we come back to the problem of performance. Expectations as to performance, by stockholders and boards of directors as well as by lenders, do have some relevance to the survival of Number One, the manager. Obviously, Number One's expectations as to Number Two's performance are relevant to the latter's survival, and so on down the hierarchy.

Expectations are strongly influenced by what has occurred in the recent past. They commonly call for performance a bit better than last year's figures, adjusted for expected business conditions or other circumstances, and for anticipated performance of the industry of which an enterprise is a part.

Maximizing the performance of an organization is not, therefore, in the best interests of the organization's management.

Continuously trying for maximum performance means disturbing fluctuations—upward profit jumps in good years when they can be made, and sudden declines in bad periods when profits fall. This is bothersome—to boards of directors, to stockholders, to the price of a company's stock, and to managers who have stock options. Managers, therefore, do not always strive to show the maximum profits in every year. They try rather to maintain what is or what looks like a steady progression. In other words, *management strives to perform at expected rather than at optimal levels.*

This leads to a perhaps cynical comment, effectively a

restatement of what has already been expressed. There really may be a disadvantage, oddly enough, in trying to get additional business, or to increase profit margins, or to cut costs, once it is apparent that the year's sales and profit goals for a company will be safely met.

"I told you we don't want any more orders now. We've already met our expected goals. Save them for next year."

It can be argued that steady performance, preferably with some progression, albeit modest, has some bona fide advantage over maximizing performance, other than the survival of management. Profits will vary with competitive, economic, and political circumstances, irrespective of management ability; and striving continually to maximize them will lead to wide fluctuations in profits from year to year. The fluctuations can be somewhat tempered, evened out, if management strives for a steady, progressing flow of profits rather than the optimum each year. A steady progression, if it can be managed, makes planning a lot easier and life in general more pleasant. Drastic profit variations may lead to drastic fluctuations in personnel and programs—maintenance, advertising, research and development, management-training programs, etc.—which may be cut back when profits are low and built back up again in periods of high profit. A steady progression avoids the necessity for such inefficiencies, and may avoid undesirable effects on public image.

The loss in satisfaction to those concerned—disutility—of a given loss in profits in one year is greater than the gain in satisfaction—utility—of the same number of dollars added to profits in another year. An even flow of profits, a steady progression even more so, provides more total satisfactions than does an up-down-up-down flow, even if over a period of time the average profits are the same.

The stockholder and the banker recognize this. A steady progression of profits brings a higher price for stock, for a given average of earnings, than do fluctuating profits. Steady progression is good for raising capital, whether by selling stock or by borrowing. It is good for management survival, bonuses, and stock options.

The desire for a steady progression of profits, or the appearance thereof, leads to a number of methods for arriving at such a progression.

I. When profits are unusually high, they may be reduced.
   A. Management may increase current expense as an investment for the future in a number of ways, for example:
      1. Advertising, research and development, repairs and maintenance—all may be increased.
      2. Sales and other areas in the organization may be strengthened for the future through hiring additional personnel now and by adding to training and

development programs for workers, supervisors, and management.

3. Whether as capital and with it capital expense, or as current expense, manufacturing and warehousing facilities may be updated or added to; office space may be expanded; older furnishings may be replaced with new.

B. Management may also increase expense in other ways, though within limitations imposed by Internal Revenue and other governmental regulations.

1. In some instances, the company may be able to prepay expenses such as rent, light, maintenance costs, or other services under contractual agreements.

2. Profit-sharing and pension plans can be augmented.

3. Additions to overhead can be justified or rationalized, and do in fact tend to come about when profits are high.

4. The method of valuing inventory may be changed —first-in-first-out (fifo) to last-in-first-out (lifo) —in times of inflation.

5. The book value of obsolete inventory, plant and physical assets, patents, and goodwill may be written down.

6. Depreciation may be switched from straight-line to an accelerated basis.

   a. Depreciation is calculated under accounting rules as so many dollars each year, regardless of output. If business is good and volume high, depreciation charges per unit of output are low. If business is not good, volume is low; so depreciation costs go up per unit. Profits are exaggerated when they are high anyway; they are depressed when they are low as it is.

Thus, in a sense, accounting tradition aggravates the business cycle.

7. Reserves, as for bad debts, may be increased.
8. Operating improvements and "fat"-cutting may be postponed, perhaps not so much by conscious deliberation as by concentrating priority of attention on strengthening the organization, etc.

II. When profits are low, management can increase them.

   A. Management may cut expenses.

      1. Cuts may be made in advertising, research and development, current repairs and maintenance, travel, telephone, training programs expense, and in overhead expense generally.
      2. "Fat" and "deadwood," kept when profits are good, may be trimmed—by firing or in some cases early retirement.
      3. Priority of attention can be directed to operating improvements that have been postponed or were neglected when profits were good.
      4. Some start-up expenses may be capitalized.

   B. Additionally, management may increase profits by generating nonrecurring income.

      1. Assets that are not needed and are carried on the books at low or depreciated costs, with market value exceeding book value, can be sold off at market value, which results in nonrecurring income. The assets may be real estate, securities, film libraries, etc.
      2. Land and buildings can be sold at overstated prices. This creates a capital gain for the current year. The buyer then immediately leases the real estate back to the seller on a long-term basis at a rental that justifies the puffed-up sales price.
      3. Properties may be traded at exaggerated prices with other firms. An insurance company may have

acquired real estate on default of a mortgage. The mortgage loans made may exceed the price at which the property can be sold. The same is true for a bank. The insurance company and the bank can sell their respective properties to each other at the overstated prices. Real losses don't show up. One may even create a profit and then hope that inflation will provide a bail-out.

4. Assets may be revalued upward—patents, goodwill, and physical assets including inventory. Customary write-offs of obsolete inventory may be postponed.

5. The minerals and petroleum industries may use production payments: selling off assets still underground.

6. Inventories can be transferred to a subsidiary. The transfer can be called a sale, with profit accruing.

7. Accounting procedures can be changed to include with sales and profits the total value of goods sold on an installment basis. Although such profits actually accrue over a period of several years, they may be made to appear all in the current year.

Management may often blame losses on a previous management; or on recession; or on a government decree, as when children's clothing treated with fire-retarding "tris" was banned, with resulting heavy inventory losses. Management may then decide to go all the way in adding to losses by writing down drastically, at once, all equipment and inventories that are obsolete or near obsolete, or whose value can otherwise be questioned. It may also sell off or close down unprofitable divisions and facilities, at considerable losses. A whopper of a loss figure results, but so does an easy opportunity for showing dramatic improvement in ensuing quarters. Management looks good by comparison with what might have happened if it had not taken such action.

In a sense, in some cases, profits can be manufactured to order. Thus if an organization owns lots of real estate, large film libraries, or other assets that constitute a sort of inventory; and if book value is less than market value, undervalued assets can be sold off when and to the degree necessary to create the required amount of profit. Banks can do the same with a portfolio of securities—sell off gainers to create profit when needed; sell off losers when the losses can be offset by higher-than-needed operating profits.

To sum up, the principal objectives of management are its own survival and the maximization of its own satisfactions. The survival, progress, and performance of the organization are means to those ends, not the ends, though they may be necessary to the survival and satisfactions of management, and though they may of themselves represent some of the satisfactions gained by management.

As to an organization's performance, management's best interests are served by striving for the expected, not the optimal, outcome. This calls for results a bit better than last year's figures, adjusted for expected business conditions and for anticipated performance of the industry of which an enterprise is a part. A steady level of performance, preferably with some progressions, albeit modest, is perferred to the performance fluctuations inherent in attempting continually to achieve the greatest results.

Hypotheses:

Number One's priority is Number One.

Maximizing the performance of an organization is not in the best interests of the organization's management. Rather, management strives to perform at expected, not optimal, levels.

4

Large Enterprises Are More Efficient Than Small Enterprises

Reality: If the large enterprise is really more efficient than the small, what permits small business to exist?

The big fellow often is indeed more efficient. Thus the large enterprise gains a substantial advantage if it can use costlier but more effective equipment to produce a product. It can also have the advantages of acquiring raw materials more cheaply, advertising on national TV and thus at a lower cost per unit sold for a consumer product, and selling through a strong, nationwide organization of dealerships not available to the smaller competitor. Obviously, the very large firms can borrow at lower interest rates and minimize the cost of keeping records and filling out required forms for the government by spreading that cost over a large volume of output. The effort required to conform with governmental regulations is a burden that most definitely does adversely affect the little fellow.

However, the small firm can compete with the big where the most efficient technology available is not too costly for it to be utilized effectively. The term *technology* as used here includes, not only the narrow technical sense, but also organization, procedures, and facilities, plus management and other

*"The government wants to help you, so it's asking you
to fill out these additional forms."*

"people talent" for marketing, financing, and other support
activities.

Small companies face real problems in competing when the
scale of their operations is not large enough to utilize the most
efficient manufacturing technology available. They may face
an even greater problem when the size of their operations
won't permit them to take advantage of the most economical
and efficient marketing and financing techniques. That's why
companies even quite large by some industry standards may
have difficulties. The needs for both adequate financing and
a related strong, national system of dealerships, which are only
available to the very, very large, have made it difficult for
the American Motors Company, for example, to compete in
the automotive industry. There are literally hundreds of other

companies that face the same or similar problems arising from the size requirements for efficient marketing and financing, and not merely manufacturing.

The modest enterprise can compete, provided the optimal technology does not require large size for its effective utilization. This is true in many kinds of retail and service businesses and in some labor-intensive industries. Further, in some businesses, the little fellow may overcome in whole or in part the disadvantage of less efficient technology, since he may enjoy greater flexibility and speed in adapting to market needs, the ability to provide specialized and personal services to customers, and the avoidance of some of the high costs of red tape.

Efficiency of performance declines as size increases beyond that required by efficient technology. Difficulties of communication and red tape increase. Rigidity increases. Innovation and entrepreneurship tend to decrease.

Are profits in terms of return on capital invested then likely to be highest for the very largest firms in an industry? Or are they more likely to be larger for firms big enough to take advantage of the best available technology, yet not grossly larger than is required effectively to utilize that technology? At least some figures indicate the latter may be true.

There are reasons why an organization may grow, continue to grow, and maintain sufficient profits to survive far beyond the optimal size dictates of technology. The imperfect nature of the marketplace is one reason. The market is not free. It commonly does not operate on the basis of pure competition. Established market contacts and friendships, tie-ins, reciprocity, customer inertia, brand loyalties, patents, government regulators, illegal cartel-like understandings, implied threat of and actual price wars, and other restraints exist.

Other underlying factors also favor growth beyond optimum economic size. The desire of managers, and the tendency of corporate as of other bureaucracy to grow—Parkinson's Law —is important. Growth has rewards for those who run an organization, among them money, power, position, and prestige, and accomplishment in the game of growth. Moreover, the computer has given managers and bureaucracy the means by which highly centralized and detailed control can be extended to organizations of very large size. Very large enterprises would be more difficult to control without the information systems and massive data handling the computer can provide.

Hypotheses:

An organization's efficiency of performance declines as size increases beyond that required by efficient technology. Its optimum size is therefore the minimum size that can effectively utilize the best technology available. Technology *is used in both a technical and an organizational sense.*

The time required for an organization to adapt to needs and changes in the marketplace or elsewhere increases with the size of the organization. This is countered by economies of scale and by the synergistic effect of size on control in the marketplace.

National TV, governmental forms, and the computer all contribute to the encouragement of large firms.

5

Organization Structures in Practice Conform to Commonly Stated "Principles" of Good Management

Reality: The commonly stated "principles" of good management start with definite rules on the minimum and maximum number of subordinates who should report to one person, a clear distinction between line managers who command and staff who advise, and the premise that an individual should have only one boss.

The principles are violated often, and rightly so. Let's start with the following story, based on something that really happened, to illustrate a point relative to *span of control*—the number of subordinates reporting to one person.

A few years ago, X was hired and made vice-president of the manufacturing department of a large firm. Reporting to him was Y, who had been responsible previously for all manufacturing operations and who continued with the same responsibilities under the new vice-president. But now Y reported to X instead of directly to the president. The new arrangement seemed to work well.

Of course, after a while some within the organization began to wonder who else besides Y reported to X, and the answer was, No one! How come? Well, of course, X was a golfing buddy and also owned a boat jointly with the president—but, of course, this couldn't have anything to do with his duties as vice-president—or could it?

Subsequently the president left, after a difference of opinion with one of the members of the board of directors who also happened to be the company's major stockholder. When a new president was selected, he reviewed the duties of those reporting to him and discovered that there was really no good reason to have a vice-president of manufacturing interposed between the president of the firm and the only subordinate who reported to that vice-president, namely, the general manager of manufacturing.

For an executive, any manager, to have only one subordinate reporting to him does ordinarily raise a question of need. One subordinate only, reporting to a manager, violates a general concept of good practice, namely that a manager should have anywhere from at least three or four to not more than seven or eight subordinates reporting to him.

Yet it is not possible to generalize on the minimum or maximum span of control a manager should have. Thus it is indeed possible to have situations where, justifiably, only one subordinate reports to a superior, or on the other hand, where many, many more than seven or eight report to him. The common assumptions of what is good management may not always be followed.

For instance, a board chairman may conceivably have only one man reporting to him, the president or other chief executive officer (c.e.o.), whose responsibility is internal, the company's operations. The chairman himself could be concentrating his attention on company long-range strategy and policy, and on relations with the outside world—the government, the public, the industry, and the financial community. He could also be keeping in touch with a few major customers. In a small company the chairman could be "Mr. Outside" all by himself; in a larger company he would have staff assistance.

In a closely held organization, one owned by one or only a

few individuals, the major stockholder is likely to be the chairman. He may have only a president reporting to him, with the president handling both internal operations and relations with the outside world (inclusive of a few major customers). In that way, the chairman keeps in touch with what goes on and retains control. At the same time he is able to devote the major share of his attention to other private affairs, to politics, or to special personal interests.

The opposite of a one-to-one relationship is that where as many as a hundred or more subordinates may report to one person. An example of this is the White House. There are scores of people who in theory at least report directly to the president of the United States. Many of them may report in person only once a year, or they may report only through written summaries of the activities of their particular agency, or they may report through presidential aides—but they are at least supposed to be responsible to the president.

The number of people reporting to one person is to some degree a matter of arithmetic. How many hours does one have available for conferring with his subordinates, how often does he need to confer with each, and how much time does each conference take? To put it another way, *the number of subordinates who can report effectively to a manager is equal to the hours available to the manager for managing divided by the number of hours he requires on average to manage each subordinate.*

Highly technical, complex, and fast-changing situations obviously require considerable time per subordinate, and consequently few subordinates per superior. A greater number of subordinates can be handled by one man in a relatively simple, standardized, repetitive, and slow-changing situation.

The degree to which the top man is willing to delegate both responsibility and authority to his subordinates is also a factor in determining how many can effectively report to that man. Frequent conferences involving considerable time and a myriad of details will be required if subordinates are constantly to be told what to do. To operate effectively, to avoid bogging down, a person can then manage only a limited number of subordinates.

On the other hand, if subordinates are to be allowed and are expected to run their own shows, then less contact time is needed. In these situations only occasional reporting to and instructions from the boss are required. Each manager can have a greater number of persons reporting to him.

Indeed, one way to encourage delegation of responsibility and authority is deliberately to structure an organization so that as many as twenty or more subordinates report to one manager. With a large number reporting directly to him, a wide span of control, a manager simply doesn't have time to get into a lot of detail with all of his subordinates. He has to delegate. For this and other reasons, many companies have adopted as policy the wide span of control.

Obviously the wide span, with each manager handling a large number of subordinates, means fewer management layers are interposed between those at the top and those at the bottom of an organization. This makes for what is known as a flat or horizontal structure. The opposite is true when each manager handles only a few subordinates; more management layers are necessary. This then produces a management hierarchy that forms a steep pyramid—in other words, a vertical structure.

Let's illustrate further. A total of ten managers is needed for eighty-one junior-level subordinates if each manager handles nine persons reporting directly to him. There is a general manager and one layer of management below him composed of nine subordinates. Each of these nine supervises nine others.

On the other hand, a total of forty managers, the general manager plus thirty-nine others, forming three layers between top and bottom, will be required for the same eighty-one individuals if each manager has only three persons reporting to him. The general manager has three subordinates, composing the first management layer under him. Each of the first layer has three subordinates, constituting a second layer of nine. A third layer of twenty-seven reports to the second layer of nine. Finally the third layer of twenty-seven, with three persons reporting to each of the twenty-seven, supervises the eighty-one subordinates at the bottom.

Or one may have, as a compromise, thirteen managers, with two layers between top management and the eighty-one at the bottom; the general manager and his first layer of three managers, plus a second layer of nine reporting to the three. The second layer in turn supervises eighty-one, nine to a manager.

Other things being equal, and often they are not, horizontal structures have some advantages. They mean less overhead, and in most cases they also simplify the transmission of information and the implementation of top management's decisions. The amount of delay, misinterpretation, and distortion, even passive resistance and occasionally direct sabotage, in communicating information and in implementing orders increases with the number of command layers between top and bottom.

Let's turn our attention to line and staff relationships. Line and staff are supposed to be separate and distinct in the organization, line commanding and staff advising. Are line and staff really separate and distinct? The following story is illustrative of the blurring between the two that occurs in practice.

A plant superintendent was about ready to promote to a supervisory position a promising young man who had been with the company about five years. The personnel director got wind of it and suggested to the superintendent that he promote another instead, a woman who had been with the company only three years. The woman was qualified about equally with the young man, but she was a woman. The superintendent didn't like it, nor did he believe in women supervisors. He refused.

The personnel director then talked to the vice-president of manufacturing. Affirmative action required that women be represented in management, and there were very few women in management. The vice-president might disagree, but he

knew the personnel man had the ear of the president, so he
acceded. The next day the vice-president, who also would
have preferred the young man, ordered the superintendent to
promote the woman. This was done.

The personnel director, a staff manager, had effectively
overruled line management on a matter of promotion within
the department of manufacturing. By the conventional rules
—principles—a decision on promotion should certainly have
been the prerogative of manufacturing management.

The usual wisdom is that line commands and staff merely
supports. Thus a senior manager will delegate to line subordinates responsibility and authority to carry out the functions of
an organization or a department. Line managers are given responsibility for their areas plus authority to give orders for
carrying out the activities in these areas. Additionally, a senior
manager will delegate to staff subordinates responsibility for
planning and monitoring needed to enable the senior manager
to supervise his line subordinates. He will also delegate to
staff responsibility for matters requiring technical knowledge
and skills not possessed by the line managers; and for dealing
with outsiders other than customers—that is, suppliers, labor
unions, the public, and the government. Manufacturing is a
line function. So is sales. Finance, engineering, and personnel
are staff functions.

Line makes command decisions and issues operating orders.
It has direct responsibility for accomplishing the objectives of
the organization. Staff advises, interprets information and
orders, and monitors.

It has been commonly assumed that staff managers have no
line authority except over those individuals who work directly
for them in carrying out their staff duties. However, they can
and do issue technical directives that line managers are
obliged to follow. They also have the authority to require of
line managers information to enable staff to monitor what goes
on. For example, the head of the personnel department, a staff
function, has the authority to draw up standards governing a

line manager's hiring employees and procedures he must follow in their discharge. Some personnel heads actually share line's authority to hire and fire.

Again, the controller, a staff manager, can demand of line managers information relevant to financial and budgetary matters. The manager of quality assurance, also staff, has line-type authority to shut down a line operation when quality of output does not meet approved standards.

Although the practice violates accepted principles, one should also recognize that staff do often wield considerable line authority informally, by reason of their influence with the senior executives to whom they report. Thus the controller, because of his influence over the budget and senior executives, may virtually dictate what capital equipment will be purchased by the manufacturing department, or how many employees the sales department will add in the coming year. Informal line authority by staff may go even further. Take for example an aggressive assistant to the president, a staff man. He may be able actually to determine who of two candidates gets promoted to assistant sales manager, when really such a decision should be left to the discretion of line, the manager of the sales department.

One can sympathize with the line manager who addresses a staff assistant and is told that their mutual boss, the senior line manager, is too busy to see the line man, but that he, the staff man, has already discussed the matter of concern. Much to the irritation of the line man, the staff assistant then proceeds to pass on the instructions purportedly issued by the boss. The line subordinate never really is quite sure how much of the instructions are the boss's and how much simply those of the staff man.

There is a lot of grey in the black-and-white separation of line and staff responsibilities and authority. In matrix organization, described in chapter 7, it is not even clear which managers are line and which staff.

Another myth in past years has held that, under good organization, a person should have only one boss. This is not completely true. In actual practice *a man does not work for one boss alone.*

Staff as well as line may be boss. The personnel department may hire or fire a production worker, separately from or jointly with the foreman. In a sense, both are the worker's bosses. Or a foreman may be boss, but the industrial engineer who sets work standards for the foreman's department is also boss. And so is the quality assurance manager who can shut a line down.

A plant manager certainly has more than one boss. He has to report, not only to his vice-president of manufacturing, but also to personnel, the controller, the chief engineer, the head of quality assurance, and sometimes to a number of others. Further examples of more-than-one-boss abound.

The cost accountant in a manufacturing department reports to both his plant manager and the company's controller.

The poor typist in that dreadful secretarial pool has countless bosses. If she makes the mistake of displeasing any one of them, she could be out on her ear.

A district sales manager may effectively be receiving orders from both his division manager and a product manager whose product constitutes 40 percent of what the district sells.

A subordinate in Department A may be told directly by the manager of Department B to provide him with some information. The manager of Department B theoretically is not the Department A subordinate's boss; yet prudence may dictate that the subordinate in Department A act as if he had two bosses.

A union employee has both his foreman and his union steward to listen to. Moreover, these two are likely to be working at cross-purposes.

As a final example, a man has both his management superior and the law to report to when he's told or allowed to presume he is to work out common pricing arrangements with the competition.

A man has only one boss to listen to. His union or his employer??

Hypotheses:

To sum up, practice deviates considerably from some commonly stated principles of good management that have been generally accepted in the past. Thus a manager's span of control, the number of people reporting directly to him, is not limited to at least three or four and not more than seven or eight people. Only one subordinate may report to a manager, or two or three or many times the presumed maximum of seven or eight may report to him. *The number of subordinates who can report effectively to a manager is equal to the hours available to the manager for managing divided by the number of hours he requires on average to manage each subordinate.*

There is a lot of grey in the black-and-white separation of

line and staff responsibilities and authority. Staff often exercises line authority. In matrix organization[1] it is not even clear
which managers in an organization are line and which are
staff.

Although an individual presumably has only one boss, in
reality he commonly has more than one boss, sometimes many
bosses. *A man does not work for one boss alone.*

---

1. See chapter 7.

6

Delegation of Responsibility Carries with It Coextensively the Delegation of Authority

Reality: *The delegation of responsibility often does not carry with it coextensively the delegation of authority.* This can lead to difficulties. The following story illustrates one kind of situation that can develop.

A company's southern region was run by a vice-president who had just received formal authorization and was responsible for getting a new plant built and ready to operate in twenty months. He did not have authority, however, to go ahead with the purchase of the required equipment before design approval by the corporate engineering staff.

The plant and equipment design had been completed by his own engineering staff months earlier. However, it had not yet been completely reviewed by corporate engineering, and obviously it had to be before a purchase order could be signed. Knowing the staff, the vice-president could only assume they would dawdle for another three months. Yet if he didn't sign a purchase order for the needed equipment immediately, the time lapse between ordering and getting the equipment, the lead time, was such that he would never get the plant operating on schedule. Moreover, with costs going up every month, he might not even get the plant built.

This was his quandary. He was, after all, a vice-president, supposedly in complete charge of his region. Getting the new plant built and the equipment installed was his responsibility. With it he should have had the authority to go ahead.

But did he? Not really. He was supposed to get corporate design approval before he ordered equipment. He hadn't received it yet, and he was realistic enough to know he wouldn't receive it within a reasonable time.

As a practical matter, if he went ahead with the procurement of equipment, and the equipment worked, there would be no problem. But if he went ahead and something went wrong, headquarters would be on his back for ordering equipment before staff had reviewed the design. If he tried to get official approval to procure equipment before design review was completed, he knew he would be told the procedural rules were inviolate. If he didn't ask, there might be rumblings about his preapproval ordering, but again, if the equipment later worked as he was sure it would, there should be no problem. This is a typical business "Catch 22" situation—damned if you do, damned if you don't.

This dilemma arose from the organizational separation between responsibility and authority that often occurs in line-staff relationships. In this particular case, a superior's low level of confidence in his regional manager might have been a factor. The superior, with or without justification from prior experience, might well have been uncomfortable in letting the region go ahead on its own before corporate staff had reviewed and approved the design.

There are many other cases where authority does not correspond with responsibility, or where authority and responsibility are in fact completely separated.

A line manager may have responsibility for the functioning of his department. Yet authority over procedures and standards may be in the hands of the personnel department; authority for spending money on overtime may be restricted by a budget over which the controller has exercised some considerable influence; and the speed at which the manager is permitted to run his assembly line may be governed by an agreement negotiated by the industrial relations department with the union.

Authority to formulate decisions on major policy, investment, and budgetary and other matters often is largely separated from responsibility for implementing those decisions.

Responsibility for reducing manufacturing cost or for increasing sales, and the authority to spend major amounts of money to do so, do not necessarily reside in the same manager. A sales manager may have responsibility for achieving a given sales volume, but the advertising budget and the promotion schedule, both important tools for him, may be completely out of his control. They may be controlled separately by a manager of advertising and promotion; or by two managers, one for advertising and one for promotion; and the budgets for advertising and promotion may have been set by the controller and the president. And of course, pricing, very important to sales, is likely also to be out of the sales manager's control. It is rarely that a president will tell his sales manager:

> We'll worry about costs later! You'll have both responsibility for meeting sales goals and authority for setting prices so you can meet them.

As can be seen, responsibility and authority often are not coextensively delegated, and should not be. A further example of this is readily seen in negotiation. Responsibility for negotiations and authority to accept or reject specific proposals commonly are deliberately separated—as with labor agreements and commercial contracts. The negotiators parley, but members of the union or a superior may separately retain the authority to accept or reject what has been negotiated.

The delegation of responsibility and authority to subordinates is supposed to preclude bypassing those subordinates.

Yet bypassing or even directly overruling a subordinate is often desirable and at times may be necessary. The following story, partially disguised, actually happened. It illustrates the direct overruling of the authority delegated to a subordinate.

The president of a firm was faced with a vice-president of marketing who wanted to fire his sales manager—the very man who was due to succeed him upon the vice-president's retirement in three months. In theory, the president was not supposed to interfere with the way a subordinate wanted to run his own department. Yet the only person who the president felt could handle the vice-president's job was the sales manager. What had turned the retiring vice-president against his sales manager? The latter had made the mistake of criticizing a protégé of his boss.

Should the president interfere? The sales manager was capable. If he were fired he would be welcomed by the competition, and a few large customers would follow him to that competition too. Needless to say, the sales manager was not fired.

Let's turn to another example, a not uncommon one that involves, not overruling, but simply bypassing, ignoring, the role of subordinates to whom responsibility and authority have been delegated.

To help retain goodwill and a close relationship, the president of a supplier firm may at times visit with the president of a customer firm. At the time of the visit he may receive a direct order for merchandise. This order has not gone through the regular sales channels. Getting that order may even have been the sole purpose of the particular visit. And the supplier's sales manager or any other sales representative may not even have known about the visit. In this example both presidents have bypassed their subordinates. One has gone over the head of his regular sales organization, and the other has totally skipped over his purchasing department.

To further illustrate, who has ever heard of a president

who, on receiving an order from an important customer on the phone, insisted:

> Your $1 million order will have to go through channels, of course! I know you need the stuff right away, but it'll take only two weeks to clear through the right channels and get to our warehouse. Then we'll ship it immediately.

In practice there is considerable bypassing of subordinates. This happens often in smaller and medium-sized firms, but it also occurs in larger enterprises.

It is sometimes important to obtain information from lower echelons through channels other than the regular line command so as to confirm information from the line that reaches the top or to make sure orders reaching the bottom are not distorted or incomplete. There can be considerable filtering through a line of command whose individual members may honestly or through personal desires and motivations misreport, misinterpret, or by shifts in nuances distort information and orders.

Communication in an organization moves downward from the top and upward from the bottom, in several ways independently of the regular line of command. Staff personnel, along with line, report directly to the top. Staff has its own independent channels of communicating within an organization. Suppose a plant manager wanted to order his cost accountant to exaggerate the value of the plant inventory of materials and parts remaining at the end of a quarter. The figures then would show fewer dollars of inventory had been used up in manufacturing than actually occurred, and thus a lower-than-actual manufacturing cost per unit of product—one within, instead of above, budgeted cost for the quarter just ended. However, the plant manager knew that the accountant reported directly to the corporate accounting department as well as to him. The accountant would be fired if it were found that he had distorted inventory value; on the other

hand, corporate headquarters would ensure his job security if
he did not follow orders to distort. The plant manager was
kept honest by his own conscience—reinforced by the accountant's dual lines of communication.

Another example of communications bypass is an internal
audit group that continually monitors both the accuracy of
data submitted by line departments and compliance with company policies. The outside accounting firm that audits a company's books provides an independent channel of communication directly to top management. An open-door policy in
listening to employee grievances, or an ombudsman who does
so, provides a bypass mechanism. An outside—sometimes inside—consultant, or a market research firm, bypasses the
regular organization structure in obtaining facts and assessing
a situation for the top.

A president may informally talk to an assembly line worker
in the company cafeteria, or to a salesman or a customer in
the field, or to a forklift operator or a truck driver at a company warehouse, or to lower echelons of the command chain—
a foreman, a junior executive, or a district sales manager—
to get a personal feel for what's going on. Written memoranda
or oral presentations by those reporting directly to him will
not always give the president this. Moreover, occasional or
regular direct bypass contacts may help to keep those who report to him "honest" and on their toes.

In theory, direct communication with lower echelons
through channels other than the direct line of command is not
necessary. A manager either can trust the honesty and ability
of the managers who report to him, or he should get new
subordinates. This is certainly true, and yet there are times
a manager must work with the people he has. It's necessary
also to remember that even excellent people sometimes,
through ignorance or misinterpretation, misreport what's going on. Communication is inherently subjective, and occasionally it is bound to be colored by touches of self-interest.

The head of one firm, a large public utility, goes so far as to have formal "skip-level" meetings. He skips below the level of the managers who report to him directly when he wants confirmation or a more complete picture of the facts, or of opinion, in a situation where he must make an important decision. Thus he will meet with a lower level of managers, or with the working level of employees in a group. The boss or bosses of that group are aware of the meeting but are excluded. The results, individual and consensus, of the ensuing bull session are supposed to be kept confidential. The top man, at least, does not reveal them to the bosses of the group with whom he has met.

While skip-level meetings may be an example of bypassing that should be practiced only with care, it is still true that *the delegation of responsibility to subordinates does not preclude bypassing those subordinates.*

It may be essential for a senior manager to give orders directly to lower echelons and workers, even at times contradicting orders given by those to whom he has delegated responsibility and authority. It may be necessary to make or implement a decision affecting a certain department while the manager of that department is on vacation or away on a business trip and either not readily reachable or not conversant with the details of a situation that requires immediate action. In such a situation it is assumed that the assistant manager, the second-in-command, is also unfamiliar with all the ramifications, for if he were it would only be good practice to let him make the decision.

Bypassing and even overruling of the command chain by a higher authority issuing direct orders, as well as engaging in direct communication with lower echelons and workers, may occasionally be good for morale of the lower groups and stimulating to the bypassed echelons. Such procedures dramatize direct communication and the correction or amelioration of very real misunderstandings, grievances, and frustrations that otherwise might never get corrected and that senior management might never even learn of in any other way. Such

situations as the unexpected departure of a capable manager
or an unforeseen wildcat strike may not actually have developed suddenly; the top simply may not have been made
aware that anything was happening.

There are such things in a chain of command, in an organization's bureaucracy, as passive resistance and even direct
violation of both the letter and spirit of orders given by the
top. Policy distortions can get covered up in a long chain of
command.

*For a system or an organization to work, it is necessary to
provide for violations of the system and the organization's
rules* in special situations. This applies to violations of an organization's structure of delegated responsibility and authority.
For example, if delivery trucks on the streets of San Francisco
were rigidly prevented from double parking, which is illegal,
the city's downtown simply could not operate. And the granting of a pardon to a president of the United States, if done to
expedite his resignation, did bypass the regular system of jus-
tice, but perhaps helped to get government as a whole to work.

The ability to delegate effectively is limited by the availability of capable people to whom to delegate. The problem
may be especially likely in a small organization. At times,
therefore, it may be desirable, even necessary, for the top to
override its subordinates, issuing orders directly over the
heads of lower-level managers who are less than completely
effective in carrying out their duties.

Special situations may arise in the nonpublic firm. If the
top manager is himself the owner, the entrepreneur who built
the business, he may sometimes find it hard to maintain the
delegating stance of an administrator in the face of his perceived need for immediate action in a crisis—and everything
to him may be crisis. Even where bypassing is not necessary,
and only the owner's ego is involved, it is his business and
prerogative.

Quick, on-the-spot action may be necessary if a manager
is to take advantage of an unexpected opportunity to tie up a

sale, even if this bypasses the salesman or district sales manager directly concerned. Similarly, an observing top executive may need to take immediate action on a safety hazard—a fire, an accident, a dangerous mislabeling, or a defective product being turned out on the production line—without waiting for the niceties of action through the regular chain of command.

Hypotheses:

The delegation of responsibility often does not carry with it coextensively the delegation of authority. The separation of line and staff may get in the way. Line may be given responsibility and partial authority, while some measure of technical authority is reserved for staff. A superior's low "comfort level" —that is, confidence in a subordinate—may also lead him to reserve for himself or for staff a degree of authority that presumably should go with a delegated responsibility. In negotiating, whether for labor or commercial contracts, the negotiators may have the responsibility for arriving at an agreement, but the authority for accepting or rejecting such agreements may rest with management or the members of a union, or the two principals for whom the negotiators are acting.

The delegation of responsibility and authority to subordinates does not preclude bypassing those subordinates. Bypassing occurs frequently in the transmission of information and occasionally even in the issuance of orders by senior managers directly to those who report to the subordinates of those senior managers.

For a system or an organization to work, it is necessary to provide for violations of the system and the organization's rules.

7

Organizational Lines of Authority and Responsibility Should Be Clear-Cut

Reality: Management theory for many years has insisted strongly on the importance of the premise that precision in organizational lines is necessary. Yet a little vagueness in defining lines of authority and responsibility, a fuzziness in the organization charts depicting them, and a bit of deliberate omission of specific description in spelling out duties are often found, and they are advantageous.

Let's start by exploring the careful spelling out of duties. What does this accomplish? Well, it is widely recognized that labor contracts do carefully spell out duties, maybe at times too much so. As a result, more manpower is sometimes needed to accomplish a task than would be the case if job descriptions —that is, work rules—were less specific and allowed for greater flexibility. The purpose of meticulously detailed job descriptions commonly is to provide either security of employment or feather-bedding—depending on whose point of view you accept.

Our graduate schools of business have had a penchant for insisting that—just as for union members—the job duties of managers be spelled out in detail. The party line appears to be the same for at least some management professors as for labor leaders. Indeed, manuals to supplement and clarify organizational charts generally include voluminous detail on duties, responsibilities, and authority, particularly in large enterprises.

An organization chart is a graphic representation of an organization's structure. Departments and positions are depicted by boxes, connected by lines of authority. Solid lines are used to show line authority—the relationship between superior and subordinate—and dotted lines to show staff authority relationships. Names of position incumbents may be included. However, in large organizations, personnel changes continually occur, so that names of incumbents are often obsolete by the time a chart is drawn up and printed.

There are some apparent advantages to clarity in organization charts and duties. In theory at least, it avoids situations where two or more people believe they have responsibilities and authority in the same areas. It avoids conflicts that may thus result. It pinpoints and therefore, it can be argued, enhances the shouldering of responsibilities. Full job descriptions make clear what is and what is not included in the work an individual is supposed to do.

The careful spelling out of duties for the lower rungs on the management ladder, the foreman or first-line supervisor, may be needed to ensure compliance with union contracts and the exclusion of such lower management from union membership. There may also be a need to clarify duties of particular individuals where safety or other requirements make clarity especially important. Detailed descriptions may also be necessary in organizations that have rigidly formalized compensation systems under which a salary raise has to be justified by adherence to job specifications. However, job descriptions as outlined on paper don't always coincide with actual work done. Descriptions may be tailored to what is needed to get a raise rather than to what really describes the job. It brings to mind the secretary who, to justify a raise, had been given the title of administrative assistant. She started to take the title seriously and had to be reminded that she was still a secretary. A year later, however, it had become necessary to convince the government that no discrimination on account of sex existed and that women did fill positions in administration and management. The secretary then had to be coached on the fact that she was now indeed an administrator.

"Remember. Your title may be Administrative Assistant, but you're still a secretary!"

In practice, despite charts and descriptions, there are areas of overlap, uncertainty and conflict in organizational authority and responsibility. Further, organizational structures sometimes are deliberately kept a bit vague. Doing so can minimize direct confrontation and the bruising and even destruction of egos and self-respect resulting from demotions of individuals and power shifts within an organization.

Vagueness—except in regard to the power and authority of Number One—is particularly found in smaller organizations. Even in large ones, deliberately or not, uncertainty as to just who is responsible for what does arise. This has been true in recent history in the federal government, for example regarding who has what responsibilities and who has what authority in certain fiscal and economic matters, trade matters, and investigations. There has been similar confusion at times in state and local governments. Other examples abound—in the private sector, the corporate sector, and in semipublic institutions such as hospitals, where the specific responsibilities or authority of the administrator and the chief of staff may be unclear. A common example is the question of just which duties, responsibilities, and authority belong to an organization's chairman, which to a president, and which to a chief executive officer, where an organization has all three. Fuzziness and overlapping in organizational relationships and responsibilities are indeed not without advantage. For example, if clarity is carried too far there may be circumstances in which a manager should act but is reluctant to do so on the grounds (sometimes excuse) that under clear organizational descriptions he lacks the authority and responsibility for action. Conversely, fuzziness, where it is feasible, gives able and aggressive managers some elbowroom for initiative. Lack of clear-cut lines may permit some managers in certain situations to overreach their authority and grab for more territory than properly belongs to them. This obviously causes friction with other managers. However, if not overdone, a little initiative and a little aggressive competition within an organizational structure may not be all bad.

Reference has already been made to avoiding the destruction of an individual manager's self-respect by making it too painfully clear he has been found wanting and has been demoted. Hence, the commonplace procedure of relieving a manager of his regular duties to free him for special assignments, or—particularly in situations where the individual has some considerable clout or following within an organization —the ritual of kicking a man upstairs—giving him a presumed promotion but fewer important duties and less real power. Clarity in such cases is not a blessing; in fact, obfuscation is almost a must.

It should be admitted, however, that the amount of fuzziness in relationships and duties that is both desirable and tolerable decreases with an organization's size. Where the restrictions of clear-cut lines and detailed duty description exist, it is not so much because they really add to management effectiveness as it is that they are a painful but necessary part of the price of bigness in an organization. The larger the organization, the more necessary does detailed clarity become. It is not an unmitigated blessing. It limits flexibility and initiative. But it is part of the price of integrating the individual efforts of many people into one overall organizational effort.

Unless the organization is very large, do organization charts and job descriptions accomplish much, except to encourage rigidity? If organizational relationships and duties are understood with reasonable clarity and appear to work reasonably well, will formalizing details on paper fill any real need, or merely lessen flexibility? Managers, as a practical matter, know the drawbacks of clarity. They do recognize the advantages of ambiguity, even while they dutifully preach the clarity they have been taught in the classroom, the seminar, or the management literature.

The dangers of formalizing structure and duties can be illustrated by this true incident, which occurred towards the very end of World War II in a South San Francisco shipyard. A group of six machinists responsible for the installation of gauges, valve plates, and identification tags of all kinds on "baby" flattops and C-3 cargo refrigeration ships was told to cease and desist fitting a copper tube extension to the gauges, because the pipe fitters' union claimed this job was in its bailiwick. Fitting the tube extension in the machinists' shop facilitated and speeded up the pipe fitters' job, but due to the rigidity of the organizational structure a jurisdictional strike was called that threw thirteen thousand machinists out of work. A certain degree of fuzziness in organizational lines would have saved literally millions of dollars and expedited the war effort.

An ad absurdum example of the dangers of formalizing structures and duties might be a supervisor telling a subordinate fighting a fire on a factory floor with a water hose:

> You can't do that! The manual says to use the fire extinguisher.

This illustration is obviously extreme and does not represent reality, but the following illustrates the situation existing a few years ago in a large corporation that prided itself on its structured organization. A personnel manager was showing a recently appointed section chief his new office. The man had been recruited from outside the company and was therefore in need of enlightenment. As they walked into the office, the personnel manager explained:

> We believe in a clearly defined organization. Notice the water pitcher on the stand next to the desk, along with the green rug and the venetian blinds. That means you're a section chief. You get two water pitchers, a bookcase, a red rug, and drapes on the windows when you become a department manager.

The traditional hierarchy, and the clear-cut delineation of authority and responsibility that theoretically goes with it, do not always work well. So-called matrix management, discussed below, represents to a large extent an attempt to overcome some of the problems that the traditional principles of good organization alone don't successfully cope with.

In the matrix management structure, two sets of managers interact. One set is comprised of the traditional functional managers, who supervise operations, marketing, and finance, along with the usual engineering, research and development, personnel, procurement, quality control, and other technical functions. But in addition, the organization includes product managers or, in high-technology and defense-related industry, program and project managers.

The functional managers provide the facilities and services needed to accomplish tasks related to the organization's product objectives or programs. In a firm producing, let us say, four major product lines, all sold to the same distribution outlets, the manufacturing manager produces for all four product managers; marketing will market for all four; similarly for engineering, research and development, etc. This avoids the duplication of facilities, people, and specialized talent that would be required for each product manager to operate his own functional department.

On the other hand, each product manager, being responsible for his own line only, will concentrate his attention on that product line. He will strive to ensure that it receives the necessary attention, effort, and priorities from the functional managers to attain the goals set for those products. He will plan and implement the necessary work breakdowns, budgets, and schedules to meet objectives on production, costs, quality, sale, and profits for those product lines.

Implementation means the product manager will do what he has to—push, cajole, threaten, bribe, or otherwise—to obtain the level of cooperation, effort, and priorities from the functional departments that will assure the meeting of his objectives. Implementation means also the continual defining and redefining of requirements; the provision of specialized expertise and help relevant specifically to his product line; and the monitoring of costs, schedules, and performance.

The functional manager implements requirements and decisions of his customers—the product or program managers. Both product and functional managers report directly to top management. Conflicts between them that cannot be solved at their own level are referred to higher management for resolution.

To a large degree matrix organization is simply an extension of line and staff management. Lines are a bit blurred, however, as to which is line—product or functional manager—and which is staff.

The structure and functioning of organizations is in a continuing state of development. There really are no hard-and-fast rules. What's done depends on the particular situation, the philosophy of the chief executive, the people involved, and the organizational history of· the firm.

Hypothesis:

The need for clarity in lines of authority and responsibility, and in the charts depicting them, increases with the size of an organization. To soften rigidity and augment flexibility, a little vagueness, a certain fuzziness, in those lines and charts is essential.

8

The Amount of Autonomy Enjoyed by an Organizational Unit Is Determined by Specific and Rational Rules

Reality: Specific and rational rules may exist. However, in matter of fact, the amount of autonomy granted an organizational unit is determined by profits and a superior's "comfort level" in dealing with his subordinates. The degree to which in general authority is centralized in an organization is influenced heavily by the amount of physical space, size of staff, and computer capacity at the central office.

We can start with the following hypothesis: *The autonomy of a department, branch, division, subsidiary, or other unit in an organization is directly related to the profit it produces relative to the profit expected of it and to a superior's comfort level in dealing with his subordinates.* One may substitute for "profit" other measures of performance—those measures that are important to the manager to whom the unit reports.

One can also postulate that management will concentrate on those subsidiaries, divisions, branches, or departments that perform poorly. These will be constantly monitored and questioned, supervised in considerable detail, and allowed minimum autonomy. They will be under the thumb of a superior authority to whom they report until performance, if need be under new managers, is satisfactory.

Factors other than performance count too. An infrequent one might be that implied in the complaint of one department head to another:

> My boss is always around checking. Aren't my profits good enough, or is it my new secretary?

In granting autonomy, one psychological factor is all-important—the comfort level of the manager to whom a subsidiary, division, branch, or department reports—for indeed this feeling will determine the amount of self-rule enjoyed. If the superior feels comfortable about a subordinate manager and his operation, the subordinate is likely to be allowed pretty much to run his own show. On the other hand, if the superior feels uneasy, or if the superior's personality is such that he feels impelled to get into the details of running even a good operation, he will limit the amount of autonomy permitted.

Somewhat facetiously, but with a modicum of truth, one should mention at least two other items as determinants of autonomy, and of the degree to which in general authority is centralized in an organization. They are computer capacity and size of staff.

The amount of computer capacity available for handling the paper work required with centralized control can determine the amount of detail called for by a manager. The greater the computer capacity, the greater the control a top manager can exercise over the operation of a subordinate, and the greater is his temptation to do just that. Increases in computer capability have been a factor in permitting growth in magnitude and complexity of organizations.

The size of staff available to monitor, question, and control an organization's activities also influences the degree of centralization. Staff often feels insecure and, to justify itself, must find fault and prove the importance of its continued survival. Continual and detailed monitoring, analyzing, faultfinding, and control are the result—to the point of absurdity, with excessive red tape, delays, and the frustration of subordinate line managers. This has happened. In at least one national organization known to the authors, divisional line managers have complained they spend more time on paperwork and back-and-forth communications with staff at the New York headquarters than they do on actually running their operation. There is something to be said for the comment made by a West Coast executive to his wife after an announcement of certain staff additions at his company's headquarters in Chicago:

> Forget about that vacation for a while. With the newly added staff at headquarters, I'll be too busy answering questionnaires and writing reports; I just won't be able to get away.

The size of a staff can depend on the amount of office space available at the head office of an organization. An organization may deliberately keep headquarters space limited for this very reason. A manager once commented directly and only half in jest that, if his company were to rent another floor in the building it occupied, he could easily justify doubling his staff, and that would mean a pretty good salary raise for him. The following represents more than pure exaggeration:

EXECUTIVE A: Do we hire a manager of space utilization?
EXECUTIVE B: That depends. Do we have office space for him?

Hypotheses:

The autonomy of a department, branch, division, subsidiary, or other unit in an organization is directly related to its performance relative to the performance expected of it and to a superior's comfort level in dealing with his subordinates.

The degree of centralization in an organization is affected by the amount of central office space available, which influences the size of staff, which in turn favors centralization; and the amount of computer capacity available for handling the data with which the staff is to keep itself busy.

9

The Board of Directors Controls Top Management, and Top Management Controls the Organization

Reality: Top management controls the board of directors, not the reverse. Also, the internal bureaucracy of an organization shares control with top management.

It is only when performance is continually poor over a protracted period that a board assumes control; even then, it is likely to keep control only long enough to initiate a change in management. When performance is reasonably up to expectations, the risk that the board will overrule the desires of management is minimal.

Increasing pressures of public opinion, implied threats of governmental regulation and inquiry, and hazards of legal liability are tending to push directors into more active participation in the affairs of the companies on whose boards they sit. Nevertheless, it is still true that management commonly controls the board rather than the other way around.

Candidates for board vacancies are commonly picked by management.

Stockholder proxies for board members to be elected or reelected are solicited, at stockholder expense, by management. Proxies for others than management or its nominees must be obtained at the solicitors' expense—though winners in anti-management proxy fights in the past have been able to vote themselves repayment.

Board members and management tend to have a community of business interests and sometimes social interrelationships—membership in the same clubs, old school ties, family ties, and so forth. Corporate presidents today are increasingly sensitive to the interrelationships of directorships and are conscious of possible conflicts. However, reciprocity is still of considerable importance. This sometimes takes the form of boards made up largely of individuals representing their own personal or organizational interests, rather than those of the stockholders of the company on whose board they sit. Thus, board members personally or through their firms may have an interest in legal, auditing, or underwriting fees; bank or insurance business; or sales of other services or of supplies and materials that the management of the company controls.

One is reminded of the president of a firm who explained to his senior vice-president:

> Johnson is going to be our new board member. He runs a trucking firm. We do a lot of business with that firm— so I think he'll be a pretty solid and dependable addition to the board.

A quotation from an article on page 1 of the *Wall Street Journal* of April 10, 1978, is relevant.

> "To achieve proper tension between a company's board and its management," adds SEC Chairman Harold Williams, "it must be recognized that there are some people who do not belong on boards—members of management, outside counsel, investment bankers, commercial bankers, and others who might realistically be thought of as suppliers hired by management."
>
> So the SEC staff is likely to recommend that the commission require more disclosure to shareowners of possible debtor-creditor, supplier-customer, investment banking, legal

counseling, and other relationships between a board nominee and the management that is proposing him. Such disclosure presumably would discourage too much coziness, whether or not it led to outright rejection of some nominees.

Again quoting from the article and surveys by Korn/Ferry International, an executive search firm:

> Korn/Ferry's count shows that 80% of corporate boards continued to be led by a chairman who is also chief executive officer—a combination that should be ended so that management won't control the agenda of board meetings, says SEC chairman Williams. Indeed, the reluctance of chief executive officers to surrender power is the reason "what we still have on boards is a bunch of their patsies, classmates and friends," contends corporation gadfly Myles B. Mace of the Harvard Business School.

A study by Spencer Stuart & Associates was reported by the *Wall Street Journal* of October 3, 1978, to have concluded that purging boards of the one hundred largest U.S. industrial companies of their corporate officers and lawyers, bankers, and other suppliers of services or materials/products would unseat 59 percent of all their directors.

It is inevitable that the bureaucracy of an organization shares in the control that top management exercises. The extent of this sharing depends on management's leadership and capabilities or lack thereof. Consider how top management arrives at its policies, decisions, and commands. Subordinates, line and staff, provide top management complete or partial, real or distorted, facts and figures, interpretations of data, and recommendations for policy and directions. Further, the subordinates, constituting the bureaucracy, carry out policy and direction. Finally, the bureaucracy provides the data by which the top judges the effectiveness of a policy, a decision, or even of a bureaucrat. The following instructions of a department head to his new and naive assistant are not without precedent:

This may be what the top brass wants! It's not what this department wants. Remember that!

Size of organization is also a factor. The larger the organization the greater is likely to be the control exercised by the bureaucracy.

Some comments on the hierarchy of management may be in order.

The hierarchy in an enterprise is likely to be a self-perpetuating one. By and large, its members pick their own successors. Thus a department manager promoted to the management of a group of departments is likely to have a major voice in selecting his successor. The same is true of a chief executive officer.

In large public companies, promotion within the hierarchy is likely to be the result of hard work and ability. It is a myth, however, to assume that promotion is the result only of hard work and ability. For each rung up the corporate ladder, there are more people of ability who work hard than there are vacancies to fill. This is especially so the nearer one gets to the top. Style, an ability to communicate, timing, other circumstances, politics, and who one knows also count.

Timing includes such factors as what spot happens to open up when, or what kind of manager is at that time needed for the particular spot, or where a person happens to be—geographically and in terms of availability and exposure—in relationship to the selector who is to fill the spot.

Ability counts, and presence or absence of ability may not be difficult to ascertain, but determining the degree of such ability and ranking several prospects for a promotion are highly subjective. The inclination of an executive or manager to favor as his successor someone whom he personally knows is therefore very important. As the president of a forest products company once stated, he owed his progress up the corporate ladder to the fact that he was lucky enough to be working continually with people who got promoted—so he got promoted. His more than half-serious advice to M.B.A. candidates aspiring to the top was to pick the right boss—someone who was going places. The boss's subordinate was bound to go places with him.

Not dissimilar advice on getting to the top is to pick the right school. The school tie does have some significance in certain firms. There are companies noted for favoring as management trainees and promotees the graduates of a specific school. Admittedly, too, there also are a few organizations that tend to avoid those same graduates for fear, rightly or wrongly, that they are too aggressive and expect too much upward progress too quickly.

In closely held firms, those in which a major share of the stock is in the hands of one or a very few individuals or families, the who-you-know factor in promotion is likely to translate into, 'Whose son or in-law or other relative are you?' This occasionally happens even in large, publicly held firms. The large firms tend, however, to operate with antinepotism policies, despite a Watson's succeeding Watson at IBM and a Sarnoff's succeeding Sarnoff at RCA.

Even where nepotism is against policy, there are exceptions. For example, in one large retail chain the board chairman's son-in-law was the president. Incidentally, that organization also had a mandatory retirement age of sixty-five for everyone, including the son-in-law. However, the eighty-three-year-old chairman was specifically exempted in the corporation's by-laws.

Promotions within an organization generally go to the organization's own people. However, selection may be from the outside if the company lacks competent personnel or confidence in its own. Moreover, a new president or other major executive may be chosen from the outside for quite other reasons. There may have been a change in the ownership or control of major blocks of stock. An injection of new blood may be desired after a period of continuing poor management performance, or to strengthen public or investor confidence. There may be a desire to acquire personnel who can influence government regulatory or purchasing agencies. Former U.S.

cabinet officers, agency heads, generals, and the like seem to get picked for top industry posts more often than would be justified by their sheer abilities alone.

Selection from inside an organization provides the advantage of knowledge: the person chosen is familiar with the company's operations, and the company knows the selectee's strengths and weaknesses. On the other hand, selection from outside has the disadvantage of uncertainties and possibly unpleasant surprises. An individual's image outside his own organization may differ markedly from that held by those who work closely with him over an extended period. Specific research findings on manager image have shown this, and common sense tends to verify it.

In filling vacancies from the outside, and sometimes in promoting from within, an enterprise should be cautious about hiring someone who has held many jobs, each for only a short time. A job hopper may have turned in good short-run performances but neglected longer-range problems and left the company before the consequences became evident—or before his superiors had fully recognized what his sensitivities told him: that he had reached his "Peter" level of incompetence. Of course, in all fairness, the job hopper may have been too superior and capable for his previous jobs.

Though now less true than formerly, it is still a fact that many companies treat lower-echelon managers quite differently than they do the high ranking. The double standard applies not only to sex, but also to tolerance for incompetence, retention of the alcoholic, severance pay after firing, and other matters. Treatment may depend upon how high up a person is in the hierarchy.

A hot argument with a foreman twenty years with a company, who may have overrun last month's budget by $5,000, can more easily lead to his firing than will some stupidity by a vice-president that costs his company $1 million. There may be morale and public relations reasons for desiring to cover up the stupidity. Yet the double standard for the hierarchy is also a factor: the vice-president is a colleague, a member of the "club"; "there, but for the grace of God go I."

Hypotheses:

The degree of control exercised by a board of directors varies inversely with the board's perception of management competence. In its own view, management is always competent.

The bureaucracy of an organization shares control with top management. The degree of that sharing varies inversely with the strength of top management's leadership and its administrative capabilities, and directly with the size of the organization.

The hierarchy picks its own successors and only in part on the basis of ability.

10

The Individuals Who Manage an Organization Work for Common Goals in the Management of That Organization

Reality: Who hasn't heard of four vice-presidents all eyeing the president's vacant chair? Do they have a common goal? Yes, but no!

An organization is made up of individuals, each with his own goals. These goals, all reflecting diverse interests, may also conflict with those of the organization.

Within the management group, the stronger the manager the higher is likely to be the priority of his personal goals. Yet he must attempt to transmute his personal goals to those of his organization. Somehow, achievement of the organization's objectives must fulfill or at least be consistent with his own individual goals. This is important to a manager's equanimity. It can't always be done, and to the degree that the two sets of goals clash all forms of frustration may arise. This is part of the price of organized effort.

Opposing interests among the different managers within an organization can be disruptive. The right measuring sticks can help to minimize opposing interests, such as those of one department versus another. Each department head wants to look good, if need be, regardless of what this does to others. Thus a manufacturing manager wants to keep costs down even if this means eliminating variations in the product. The sales manager wants sales volume, and if this can be obtained by special product variations, never mind what this does to manufacturing costs. A management information program set up to aid the forecasting of sales and thus improve manufacturing scheduling may result in substantial company savings. However, setting up the program, unless separately budgeted, may also mean a heavy charge against the budget of the finance department that funds the computer section. Resistance by the finance department to the development of the program is understandable in this situation: the cost would come out of finance's budget, and the money saved would only show up in manufacturing's performance. The respective managers' interests do not exactly coincide.

Setting up the right measurements to minimize opposing interests, therefore, is all-important. Actual costs in a manufacturing department can be compared realistically with budget if allowances are made for differing mixes of product and product variations. Performance can be better measured on that basis than on simple overall cost per unit. A sales manager can be measured by his dollar contribution to overhead and profit, above the base cost of manufacture. This will make him cognizant of volume, price, and manufacturing costs—all three. Thus if greater variation of product produces a greater contribution, that is the way he will go, but at the point where product variation entails greater added costs than added revenue, he will draw back.

If a production department is measured by output per hour, not quality, and quality control is measured by how many defective parts get through, there will be conflict. Let the production department be measured by both output and quality. Let the quality control department be measured by how few defective parts are produced as well as by conformance of the product shipped to quality standards. Then the production and the quality control managers will find it to their mutual interest to work together. This assumes, of course, that neither one is stubborn, completely self-centered, tactless, power-hungry, or impossible to work with.

Strong managers tend to place a high priority on their personal goals. Yet an enterprise requires conformity, and the greater its size the greater is the conformity required. The necessity for conformity, for administrative compromise, and at times for compromise with mediocrity discourages deviation from the established. With time, because conformity is important, a manager's personal pattern of thinking and his approach to problems tend to be channeled into conformance with his company's established pattern of thinking and its approach to problems or the public. The mannerisms or dress of his colleagues, the third martini at lunch, or anything else also will eventually be copied.

The need for conformity discourages the initiative and innovation that, at least in the long run, should be the lifeblood of a vigorous enterprise. The requirements of conformity impose both direct and subtle restraints on the individual, on his personal freedom, actions, and aspirations, and sometimes affect his spouse as well. Is this desirable? Is it part of the price of organized effort? These are real and vital questions.

Nevertheless, despite the need for conformity, the individual as a unique person may be essential to his organization. The direction, the tone, and the success of even a very large company are likely to be set by one or two, or commonly not more than three or four, individuals at the top of its hierarchical pyramid. Paradoxically, these individuals may be nonconformists who got to the top by being mavericks good enough or lucky enough to have gotten away with it.

Hypothesis:

Conflicts of interest exist between a manager and both his colleagues and his organization. Their resolution—that is, conformity to common organizational goals—is essential to the success of the organization. Nevertheless, the progress of that same organization may be directly proportional to the degree of nonconformity of a very few at the top. The maverick has his place.

11

Participative Management Is More Effective Than Autocratic Management (The Orange Shirt Principle)

Reality: An administration that is basically autocratic in outlook is commonly referred to as Theory X management. On the other hand, management that is basically participative in nature, encouraging subordinates to take part in the discussion and solution of problems, is commonly termed Theory Y management.

Most people have unstimulating jobs. For those jobs—which will continue to exist for some time as matters are now organized—Theory X management, if perceived to be able and fair, is more effective than Theory Y management.

To give two possibly extreme but illustrative examples, neither the fire chief fighting a fire nor the surgeon in the middle of an operation is likely to pause to suggest to either firemen or nurses:

Wait! We've got a problem! Let's discuss what to do next.

For some situations and jobs, however, Theory Y management is preferable.

Where Theory Y management will not significantly decrease the ability to compete, it should be adopted, regardless of whether it is actually more effective. It ought to be favored on the grounds that it is more people oriented and consistent with a democratic society, rather than simply on the grounds of managerial effectiveness. The latter may be difficult to prove or disprove. The former is a matter of philosophy.

Theory X assumes that management must use persuasion, rewards, and punishment to force behavior that will conform to the needs of the organization. Supposedly, without management direction and control, subordinates would be passive and even resistant to those needs. The theory, its critics claim, implies that people are lazy, lack ambition, dislike responsibility, don't care about organizational needs, are resistant to change, and prefer to be led rather than to make decisions and to take action on their own. There is also an implied belief in the gullibility of people and the ability to manipulate them to accomplish organizational ends.

Theory Y is more democratic in its outlook. It is basically participative in nature, encouraging subordinates to take part in the discussion and solution of the problems of an enterprise. It assumes that people generally have the capacity and a desire to work for common organizational goals. Management's job, therefore, is to provide an environment that will permit people to achieve at least some of their own goals through directing their efforts towards the objectives of the enterprise. The adherents of Theory Y believe that if people are passive or resistant to organizational needs it is because experience with X-type management has given them cause to be so.

Make no mistake though. Even with Theory Y there is a need for direction. The boss is still boss, and management is still only as good as the direction given by the boss. Consensus is not always possible, and when it is, it may represent, not good direction, but less adequate compromise.

One should be careful not to confuse X with Y management. There are many so-called Y-type managers who are really X-type people. They give lip service to participative management. It's fashionable. They go through the motions. These ambivalent managers, consciously, sometimes not consciously, use the procedure as a manipulatory device to get subordinates to think they are involved and part of the decision-making process. Presumably, if subordinates believe a decision is their own, they will work harder to implement what in actual fact is a course of action predetermined by the boss.

Who hasn't sat in on departmental or other meetings where the boss, having already made a decision, says something like "We are all democratic here. What do you fellows think we ought to do?"

Subordinates are not necessarily stupid. In fact, more often than not they are quite aware of the difference between the genuine Y-Theory manager and the phony.

There are any number of professional articles touting the greater effectiveness of Theory Y over Theory X management. It has become fashionable to promote the use of the former. So one is reminded of a fable. Once upon a time in the land of Egnaro[1] a famed industrial psychologist theorized that if managers wore orange shirts as they went about the job of managing they would be more effective. A subconscious connection on the part of both managers and the managed between the color orange and a cheerful sunrise would tend to create more cheerful attitudes and these, in turn, greater creativity, productivity, and so forth. The famed psychologist published an article on this in Egnaro's leading management journal. Another well-known social scientist read the article and was impressed. He in turn incorporated the same theory in a general review of new management thinking he was writing. He was quite positive in describing the theory and quoted studies on color preferences to back it up, though these studies were less than conclusive and really not relevant.

An outstanding management consultant gave a speech to a national meeting of top management executives. He had read the two articles. On the basis of the reputations of the psy-

---

1. Orange, spelled backwards.

chologist and the social scientist, for both of whom he had a great deal of respect, he enthusiastically endorsed the proposition. The wearing of orange shirts was indeed most helpful as part of good management practice. The management executives were impressed.

Before long the orange shirt theory was widely accepted. The best managers in Egnaro began to wear orange shirts. When Egnaro's outstanding graduate school of business conducted a study that compared good managers to poor, it found that the good managers, those who read management journals and kept up with the latest in good management practice (including the wearing of orange), generally did wear orange shirts as they went about the job of managing. The poorer managers, those who never bothered to read management journals, did not, on the other hand, wear orange shirts. Thus the "orange shirt theory" was substantiated and became the "orange shirt principle."

To some degree this is the situation with the common assumption that participative, Theory-Y management is more effective than autocratic, Theory-X methods. It may be so, and in many situations it likely is so, but the assumption's general applicability has not been proven. On the contrary, Theory X is probably more effective than Y in the majority of cases, although proof is very difficult. Neither sufficient observations nor adequate controlled experimentation can be cited to prove the general applicability of either X or Y.

Given such evidence as exists, there are indications that Theory Y is more effective than X where procedural uncertainty exists and where initiative, creativity, and/or a willingness to accept change is important. A participatory approach in dealing with subordinates is advantageous especially with middle- and higher-level management, in research, in professional and technical work, and with personnel who have dealings outside the organization, with customers, vendors, labor unions, regulatory agencies, or the public at large.

On the other hand there are strong indications that autocratic, X-type management may be more effective, with certain exceptions, in situations involving hard physical labor, highly distasteful work, or repetitive, standardized work that calls for little initiative or creativity. The X approach is preferable also in situations requiring quick decisions, especially where survival is at risk, as on a ship, on the battlefield, in surgery, and in fighting a fire. Theory X tends similarly to be followed where there is a profit squeeze and the survival of either the organization or the existing top management is endangered.

Participative management has the advantage, where it is relevant, of encouraging contributions in knowledge and ideas towards the solution of a problem by those who are most immediately familiar with a situation, and by those who will be responsible for implementing any action to be taken.

For example, the blue-collar worker on a packaging line can be helpful to the engineer designing an improved version of the equipment if the engineer is humble enough to accept ideas from one who has actually worked with the present machinery. The worker knows what works well and what doesn't.

In formulating ideas and planning for a sales campaign, participation by subordinate sales supervisors is an essential ingredient to success.

In research and development, and in professional and technical work generally, scientists, engineers, or others concerned must of necessity participate in discussions, whether on how to unscramble a molecular structure or how to solve an engineering or a legal problem. On the other hand, selection of the problems to be worked on may involve, wrongly in some cases, only top management and the manager of the professional or technical group.

Participatory decision making requires ample time for its implementation. This costs money, whether in time lost in the marketplace, opportunities lost through delay in action, or simply man-hours that could have been devoted profitably to other things. Costs should not exceed the values produced by participation. The values may be in dollars, in training and development of people, or simply in satisfying human desires. Y-type participative management, if it is genuine, can more quickly develop the potential and enlarge the understanding of an able subordinate than will the X approach.

However, the sword is double-edged. Participative management can be carried to the point where the subordinate realizes his superior is no abler, maybe even less so, than he is himself, with the ultimate result that he may come to the realization that the opportunities with his present organization are limited. Participation, therefore, may encourage the abler managers of an organization to seek employment elsewhere. Of course, if opportunities do exist internally, it may also keep them in the fold by increasing their awareness of in-house possibilities.

Participative management can lead to a superfluity of committees and distractive, not-always-so-fruitful discussions. Carried to excess, it can destroy unified direction in an organization. Further, there is no denying that decisions and actions must be made promptly when necessary. Participative decisions must be consistent with overall strategy, policy, and budgets, and Y management should not be allowed to prevent required promptness in making decisions. Participation must not be allowed to deteriorate into debilitating wrangling, or into a misconceived search for continual consensus or compromise.

Participative management by its very definition includes subordinates along with their superiors in discussions related to making decisions. In the right situation and under the right conditions this is good. It can be most helpful with a superior who really believes in participative management and subordinates who feel secure enough to participate honestly and freely.

However, an open ballot and open voting are not the same as a secret ballot and secret voting. The former leave room for what the latter are intended to prevent—intimidation and voting not in accordance with one's real desires. So it is with Y-type management. The ideas and opinions expressed by a sub-ordinate may represent, not his own, but those he thinks the boss wants to hear. To prevent this, participants need to communicate honestly. They should not feel threatened because of what they say or what they fail to say.

Participation by any individual ought generally to be limited to subjects and situations relevant to his area of operation and interest, and to discussions to which he can effectively contribute because of his abilities, knowledge, intelligence, or experience.

A lot of people, including managers, feel uncomfortable, perhaps incompetent, discussing management problems, alternatives, and decision making outside their own immediate niche. And not everyone wants to participate in solving management problems or making management decisions, even those that directly affect him. Many people have been conditioned culturally and by experience, even in America, to expect to be told what to do. Switching to a situation where they creatively participate in deciding what to do may be very difficult for them. This may be so even for a few M.B.A.s—brash as some of them are. They may expect to continue to be told, as in school, what work assignments are to be completed by what dates; and to continue properly to regurgitate what they're told is correct—whether by the professor in school or the boss at work. Switching from the management mode expected, particularly if this occurs suddenly, can create major problems.

X-type autocratic management, assuming such management to be competent, has the advantage of giving subordinates clear-cut direction. Most people, including a goodly share of middle- and lower-level managers, may actually prefer the autocratic approach, if it's reasonably rational and fair, to that which they may view as a less-decisive participative style of management.

A large part of the waking life of most people has to be spent doing things they don't particularly like. Through three years of research and a great many interviews for his book *Working,*[2] Studs Terkel found that most people hold jobs that "make them sick." They "suffer headaches, backaches, ulcers, alcoholism,drug addiction, and even nervous breakdowns, all because they find their work unsatisfying and consider it another form of violence."[3] These findings may be disputed by some opinion polls, but an examination of poll results indicates that, at the least, most people are not ecstatic about their jobs. They may adapt to them in order to gain the means for subsistence or, if they live in affluent societies, the means to acquire some of the things they don't need but want. Most jobs are not loved, nor is it likely that industry generally can soon be restructured to bring about a love relationship between the employee and his job.

In the circumstances, can we really expect people to want to participate in discussions and decisions on, for example, how to get their jobs done better, especially if by doing so they may be eliminating the job and "self-destructing"?

Participation with its attendent effort and implied responsibility for what comes about has its drawbacks. Moreover, true participation may take away the privilege of griping about decisions and actions by superiors, as an outlet for occasional frustrations and feelings of inadequacy.

When a company finds it is losing money, arbitrary cost cutting, generally accompanied by X-type management, becomes a likelihood. The cost cutting can produce fairly prompt improvement in earnings, though it can be expensive in the long run. However, it is better for the company, or at least for the existing management, to survive now and have the opportunity to recoup later than not to survive at all.

The fact of at least temporary quick improvement in earnings in a financial squeeze, following on and associated with

---

2. Studs Terkel, *Working: People Talk about What They Do All Day and How They Feel about What They Do* (New York: Pantheon Books, Inc. 1974).
3. As reported in *Parade,* January 27, 1974.

an X-type management and arbitrary action, raises a question. Does not an ambitious executive, one who is likely to have domineering tendencies anyway, get ahead faster in a large organization by quick, short-run improvement in the performance of the subunits he bosses, using X-tpye management? Do the quick results obtained mean continual quick promotion from one subunit to another, larger one? If later, because maintenance costs were unduly shaved or "people capital" and market goodwill destroyed, the roof caves in on a subunit he has left, does his company merely have further proof of how good that manager had been in producing profits compared to his successor, say a Y-type manager, who is left with some expensive pieces to pick up?

In other words, who personally is going to get ahead faster, Mr. X or Mr. Y?

The kind of leadership exercised by management can vary in degree from X to Y. There are a fair number of shades of grey between the black and white of the two. Thus, in identifying problems, considering alternatives, and making decisions, we may have the following management styles:

1. The superior makes the decision and announces it.
2. Same as 1, but the superior tries to "sell" it. Subordinates are likely to have an opportunity to ask questions.
3. The superior makes the decision tentative, subject to change if the subordinates can convince him to change it.
4. The superior identifies the problem, subordinates suggest one or more solutions, then the boss makes the decision.
5. The superior identifies the problem plus the restraints within which a decision must be made, such as a dollar limit on expenditures, and directs the subordinates concerned to make the decision as a group, with or without himself as a member. The restraints may be either the superior's or those of the manager to whom he in turn reports.

The kind of leadership that is likely to be most effective will vary with the manager, his subordinates, the situation, and long-run objectives.

A manager's personal philosophy is involved. How much emphasis does he place on the personal growth of his subordinates, the maximization of company profits short-run or long-run, and so forth? The confidence he has in his subordinates, his comfort level in sharing management decisions with them, and his sense of personal security will also bear on the administrative approach he pursues.

Whether his subordinates prefer X or Y may be a factor. Their preferences will depend on their knowledge and experience, the amount of direction they feel they need, what they have come to expect, their readiness to assume responsibility, and their interest in and identification with the boss and his problems.

Circumstances will affect the kind of leadership that is most productive. The determinants include how well people work together, the nature of the decisions to be made, and the existing time pressures. Also important is the degree to which jobs and duties are structured and the frequency and importance of change. The more structured the organization, the more likely is X management to be favored. The more there is change, the more advantageous is Y management.

The best type of management will vary with each enterprise, with each operation, and with each department. Thus, certain physically exhausting plant operations may best be run by an X-type management, while research laboratories require a Y approach. Other areas may find X, Y, or an in-between approach most desirable.

The pursuit of creative research and the suppression of creative accounting require different approaches. So do the encouragement of initiative in sales approaches and the discouragement of variations in inspecting for quality.

Timing makes a difference. One kind of manager may be desirable at one period in the history of a company or a department, and another at a later period.

Finally, there really is no one perfect management style. No two managers are exactly alike in their approach to the job of management. Despite anything said above, in reality one should recognize that, given the same kind of operation with the same kind of subordinates in the same general situation, two different types of managers may very well both be successful, or both may fail.

Hypothesis:

Most people do not have stimulating jobs. For those jobs— which will continue to exist for some time as matters are now organized—autocratic (Theory X) management, if perceived to be able and fair, is more effective than participative (Theory Y) management.

12

Secure and Happy People Are More Productive Than the Insecure and the Unhappy

Reality: The opposite tends to be true.

A link between happiness/security and productivity has been a direct and implied assumption of behavorial scientists, but they themselves have begun to raise questions about it. Its universality, at least, is of dubious validity.

Does a sense of security encourage productivity? Yes, undoubtedly, in some cases. Yet one can postulate that, on the whole, *secure and happy people have less incentive to work hard and to produce than do the insecure and the unhappy.* Do civil-service-type rules and the belief that one is secure in one's job really increase the productivity of government workers and their nonelected civil-service-governed managers? Not really!

Something akin to civil service also exists in private industry. Many companies, particularly large ones, provide virtual job security for those workers and for at least lower-echelon managers who have achieved adequate seniority status. The security frequently doesn't appear to add to productivity. Nor does perceived security of employment in good times, with plenty of alternative jobs available, necessarily add to the intensity with

*"Cutting short your coffee break again? People never
get fired here, you know."*

which some people perform on a job. Indeed, have there not
been cases, perhaps extreme, of individual managers going
so far as deliberately to fire a few people each year to create
uncertainty and insecurity and thereby increase productivity?

Does happiness, better defined perhaps as contentment with
one's situation, add to productivity? Or, on the contrary, is
it the dissatisfied, the unhappy individual who wants improvement in his situation and is therefore likely to strive to get that
improvement? After all, why knock yourself out working
hard to achieve if you're happy with what you already have, or
to get ahead if you're content with the position you now hold?
How often are happy angels in heaven depicted as working
very hard, that is, being productive?

Consider the inhabitants of some Pacific islands who were encouraged to collect coconuts—in other words, to work hard, far harder than they had ever worked before—through an appeal to their personal unhappiness. This was achieved by fostering a desire for goods brought in by traders and led, of course, to excellent business for the merchants. Previously, the islanders had been as happy without these goods.

Similarly, today some people moonlight and many wives work to pay for bigger-than-needed homes. Like the islanders, they were made unhappy with smaller homes through advertising and salesmen pointing to what "Jones" possessed.

Upper-level managers who have upgraded their incomes and concurrently their expenditures—for bigger homes with bigger mortgages, the appropriate furniture, and the country club—often work pretty hard. They need their salaries to pay for acquired tastes. They also feel a compulsion to keep up with the living standards of their managerial colleagues. However, they are not necessarily truly happy.

Productivity may increase, often does increase, if pressure for production is exerted. Yet as such pressure is exerted on employees, happiness on the job is likely to decrease. On the other hand, when an assembly line is slowed happiness may increase, or at least unhappiness decrease—but productivity goes down. Regardless of all these considerations, there is something to be said for security and happiness. They are both desirable people goals. We are supposed to be living in a period when humanistic goals are considered worthwhile.

It is true that, even from a productivity viewpoint, security and happiness or satisfaction have some advantages in some kinds of jobs. A sense of security lessens resistance to change. Resistance makes change difficult, and passive resistance arising from insecurity, real or merely perceived, can especially be a problem, as most managers know.

The following hypothesis can be formulated: *Passive resistance is directly proportional to the amount of perceived insecurity.*

Perceived insecurity may be due to fear of adverse change in employment or duties; inability to carry out different or enlarged responsibilities; or lack of knowledge or training. Employees may distrust management motives or have other reasons for feeling insecure.

A sense of security can lead to greater concentration on the work to be done, and hence increased productivity, by those who are fortunate enough to have an interesting and challenging job.

People who are happy or at least satisfied with their job situation are less likely to want to quit. Turnover, with its attendent costs of training and initially low productivity, should be less than with unhappy people. Quality of output, too, should be higher, and error and accident rates lower.

Satisfaction or happiness with the job, as well as a sense of security, can be advantageous for work requiring a large measure of initiative and creativity.

The relationship between performance and happiness or job satisfaction in different kinds of jobs needs further study and, in a broader sense, so does the whole area of motivation, about which we know less than would be indicated by the volume of literature on the subject.

Most jobs in our industrial society can provide only limited satisfaction for the people performing them. The situation is likely to continue for some time. Therefore large numbers of people hold jobs that are in a real sense demotivating. They spend a good deal of their waking life doing things they don't particularly like doing, in order to gain the wherewithal to do things they like to do better.

Even advertising on TV today recognizes that people do things they're not really enamored with, just so they can get to do things they like. Arnold Palmer recommends using a Lanier pocket tape recorder, but in the end he says as he is hitting a golf ball down Wall Street, "It leaves me more time to do the things I like to do."

A 1977 poll by Opinion Research Corporation of Princeton, New Jersey, indicates that more American workers were then dissatisfied with their jobs than at any previous time in twenty-five years of polling. The poll found that 32 percent of current clerical employees and 38 percent of employees paid on an hourly basis were unhappy with the work they did.[1] The figures presumably could be much higher, depending on how questions were worded and interpreted, how sampling was done, how interviews were conducted.

The figures also refer to the dissatisfied. Even if 32 percent or 38 percent were dissatisfied, that does not mean that 68 percent or 62 percent respectively were satisfied. A large portion of the 68 percent or 62 percent may represent accommodation —by people who never expected much or whose expectations have been diminished by socialization and work experience, and who have thus come to an acceptance, not necessarily with enthusiasm, of the work they do. They work at their jobs with indifference rather than any real satisfaction. Their interests and their real satisfactions lie in off-the-job activities. Moreover, both psychological and social conditioning leads many people to say they are satisfied when in truth they are not.

A national survey by the University of Michigan's Institute for Social Research, released to the public by the U.S. Labor Department in December, 1978, compares results for 1977 with those for 1973 and confirms an apparent decline in job satisfaction.[2]

Managers are less likely than clerical or hourly workers to be dissatisfied with their jobs, although many are. Among the stronger motivators for managers is the challenge of achievement, of meeting and solving problems. Problems, deviations from routine, can keep a manager stimulated. This is particularly true if he is high enough in the organizational hierarchy

---

1. *San Jose Mercury,* August 10, 1977, p. 66.
2. *Wall Street Journal,* December 18, 1978, p. 35.

to feel that the problems he meets are significant and that he himself can contribute meaningfully to their solution.

However, even at top levels in the hierarchy, challenge decreases with the passage of time in the same job in the same organization. Through meeting a repetitive flow of essentially the same or similar problems, a manager can go stale. Managers who bring a fresh approach and different experiences and viewpoints to problem solving can benefit an organization. Turnover, in other words, can be an asset as well as a liability; continuity of experience can be a liability as well as an asset.

A change in jobs, perhaps every five years or so, and perhaps even in careers, say every ten to fifteen years, may be good for the individual and for the organization that employs him. This is possible for the few. It is not now, nor is it likely soon to be, feasible on a wide scale.

Some years ago, D. Stanley Eitzen and N. R. Yetman studied college basketball team records and found that length of coaching tenure affects team performance. On an average, the longer the tenure of the coach the greater was a team's success, but after tenure of thirteen years or so effectiveness went down.[3]

Retirement, until recently generally mandatory at sixty-five, has provided one means for forcing change; turnover provides the incentives of higher-ranking positions opening up to the young and brings new viewpoints to the organization.

Job rotation is a means of creating interest, challenge, and freshness. However, with today's highly specialized work requirements, rotation can be difficult. Moreover, it is expensive and produces few immediately discernible results. Rotation, when practical, is mostly horizontal. Vertical rotation is not nearly as common. It could be useful to both the individual and the organization, but it is not likely to be widely adopted. Number Two or Number Three may not object to

---

3. D. Stanley Eitzen and Norman R. Yetman, "Managerial Change, Longevity, and Organizational Effectiveness," *Administrative Science Quarterly 17* (March 1972): 110–16.

rotation to the Number-One spot, even for only a short tour of duty, but Number One is not likely to welcome stepping down, even temporarily.

Vertical rotation does take place, in a sense, when a line manager in a lower hierarchical echelon gets moved to a staff position dealing with higher-echelon management, and the reverse. Thus, a branch manager in the field may be moved upward into a position as a staff assistant to a senior vice-president at corporate headquarters, to broaden his experience and outlook, and then moved back down the line as the regional manager of several branches.

Performance is affected by expectations, which of themselves constitute a motivating factor. In a sense it can be said that *performance is directly related to the level of expectations and desire—providing the expectations are within the limits of what physically and otherwise can be accomplished, and the desire is sufficient to bring out the required effort.*

Expectations play a wide role in the setting of objectives. Thus, they play an important part in determining budget levels, whether for overhead such as general and administrative expense, or for research and development, or for advertising costs. They are an important factor in setting sales quotas and profit goals, and they are an integral part of wage bargaining.

Expectations have a habit of becoming self-fulfilling. They can lower as well as raise performance. The newcomer who produces above expected levels of output because he doesn't know any better, whether blue collar, white collar, or even in the managerial class, is a threat. He is not appreciated, and he is likely to be taught quickly, sometimes quite directly, what the productivity expectations are.

Expectations help maintain a certain amount of overtime, whether needed or not. As is well known, overtime required for a while in an emergency, but continued too long, becomes an expectation. It gets to be a habit—with pay for the worker to whom the overtime incomes becomes a right, or without pay for the executive who comes into the office early or stays late and sometimes even comes in Saturday mornings. A la Parkinson, overtime need not increase output. The same work merely stretches to cover the available hours.

Sales quotas represent expectations of sales to be obtained, objectives on the basis of which rewards and punishments are apportioned. The same is true for profit quotas. Managers' profit goals are determined more by the expectations of the board of directors, the stockholders, and/or themselves than by a desire to maximize profits.

The role of expectations is illustrated by the experience of a young engineer on his first job over forty years ago. Time standards were initiated for work done by operators on the packaging lines in a pharmaceutical plant. Wages were to be paid for output on a piecework basis in lieu of the old hourly rate. The new standards were generally met, except on one bottle-filling line. Time standards indicated the output there could and should be doubled. For five weeks the operators continued filling on the old output basis, even though the new piece rates meant their earnings were down to half of previous levels, and during the depression of the thirties this wasn't too much. The sixth week, output suddenly doubled, and earnings were back to normal, at the new piece rates. The operators had finally accepted the thought that management was not going to back down and lower the expectations of output to the former level, so—they began to produce at the newly expected higher level.

Job enrichment or job enlargement has been promoted as a means for providing greater job satisfaction and so improving productivity and quality of output. The job is presumably made larger, less restrictive. This is more than simply job extension or the addition of similar elements, such as tightening four bolts instead of two. The theory is that as jobs become more specialized they become more repetitive, thus more monotonous, thus boring, and thus dissatisfying. When enlarged, with an increase in satisfaction, increased performance should result. That improved performance will indeed come with increased satisfaction is likely true in some cases, but not necessarily in most. Increased satisfaction is certainly a worthwhile goal in itself, but better performance through greater satisfaction has yet to be proved.

There is some evidence that people vary in their susceptibility to monotony. Some workers do not object to repetitive jobs, even those with a very short work cycle. To some, repetitive work indeed may be more pleasant than nonrepetitive work which requires constant decision making and constant change in the work rhythm. This is also true of many managers, particularly though not exclusively at lower and middle echelons.

It has been suggested that job enlargement is most likely to increase satisfaction for white-collar and supervisory workers and for blue-collar workers in rural areas and smaller communities, and less likely to affect the degree of satisfaction of blue-collar workers in the larger cities. Cultural background and value systems undoubtedly play an important role in preferences and the response to job enlargement.

Hypotheses:

We believe that on the whole *secure and happy people have less incentive to work hard and to produce than do the insecure and the unhappy.*

Passive resistance is directly proportional to the amount of perceived insecurity.

Performance is directly related to the level of expectations and desire—providing the expectations are within the limits of what physically and otherwise can be accomplished, and the desire is sufficient to bring out the required effort.

13

Managers, and Other People, Prefer Challenge to Routine

Reality: On the contrary, managers and other people often prefer routine to challenge. Stability, routine, the safety and convenience of a minimum amount of effort and thinking and a maximum amount of security are advantages not to be denied and in fact are sought by many, including managers. A rut, if it's comfortable, is not all bad.

A blue-collar worker, when offered it, may refuse the foreman's job and its headaches. The increase in pay is not really enough to compensate for the undesired challenge of the job and to entice the worker away from the comfort of a rut. It must be admitted that the offer of a foreman's job is not altogether a good example. Sometimes, with only a limited pay increase for the job and no compensation allowed for a foreman's overtime, the worker is better off even financially to turn down the promotion. Moreover, if he has seniority as a union member he has a certain security of employment. On the other hand, as a foreman he may lose the security provided by union membership and union contract rules. On top of this, the challenge of a foreman's position is often truly a headache rather than an attraction.

The middle manager too may not be attracted by challenge. He may prefer to continue living in San Francisco, Indianapolis, or Philadelphia to a promotion to a job elsewhere. The challenge of promotion is less important to him than the security of existing social relationships and life-style and the maintenance of the known and comfortable routine of the present job.

The middle-aged manager, whether at a lower or a higher echelon, may be happy in his present job. He has an unruffled routine with which he feels comfortably competent. The prospect of a promotion—with unsettling challenge, requiring new learning, new effort, new personal interrelationships, and even accompanied by uncertainties as to his own competence—is not to be considered an unmixed blessing. Yet corporate philosophy may require him to pretend he wants a promotion or a challenge that he really doesn't.

The head of an old-line family concern who is well satisfied with a stable, pleasant routine and established personal relationships with executives and nonexecutives in the company may prefer a known routine and earnings to the challenge of doubling or tripling sales volume and profits at the expense of the stability he enjoys.

The assembly line, whether blue or white or pastel collar, may be mindless and not very exciting, but—providing its pace is comfortable—the routine has its benefits.

Note that good managers work to create controllable routine, that is, to get away from less controllable challenge. The challenge of a mess is to get it cleaned up and the situation back to normal so that there is no longer a need for more than routine. When equipment breaks down in a plant, management is less interested in rising to the challenge of the breakdown than in getting the thing fixed. One is not likely to hear a plant manager comment with a feeling of joy:

> We're all fouled up again. Great! Johnson has created another challenge.

Hypothesis:

The preference for challenge varies directly with its nature and rewards, but varies inversely with reduction in the comfort provided by the routine and the established.

14

Systematic Formal Appraisals Motivate

Reality: Maybe! They also demotivate.

As organizations grow larger, and middle and lower managers become increasingly anonymous, many top managements have come to believe that better personnel decisions can be made with uniform appraisal systems. Yet appraisals are a nuisance at best and can be dangerous at worst.

"How am I doing?" Appraisals, in the form of grades, do motivate students, whether in terms of ego satisfaction or the potential rewards of promotion, entrance to college, or a better job opportunity on graduation. The same can be true for people who work and are not students. Appraisals can make people feel good about themselves. They can also serve as a basis for rewards in the form of merit raises and promotions. However, appraisals also can create resentment, frustration, and a drop in productivity where self-appraisal is considerably higher than is the boss's opinion.

How honest can appraisals be, or for that matter should they be? Can human relationships, as in a continuing job situation, tolerate absolute honesty, and for how long? The halo effect, where the boss gives his subordinates a rosier view of themselves than he himself really has, is common. The rosier-view approach makes playing the Almighty easier and a sustained job relationship more pleasant. It is not uncommon for an executive, knowing he can't get anyone better, to abstain from telling a subordinate how poor his performance really is for fear he might quit.

A manager is under continuous pressure to keep up with the merit raises other managers obtain for their personnel by giving them universal appraisal ratings of good, very good, or excellent. This works just as college averages have done for years. Grades have risen continually without regard to the actual merit of successive classes of students. Bearing on this is a *Wall Street Journal* article on formal job appraisals, May 23, 1978. Paul Knox, Republic National's vice-president for personnel, speaking of the appraisal system that his company stopped using, said there had been a tendency for managers to push up performance ratings so as not to jeopardize a subordinate's salary or career.

The granting of a raise is often the crux of the appraisal process, for both the individual being appraised and for the superior. The individual wants to know, "Do I get a raise or not, and how much?" His boss asks, "What kind of an appraisal do I come up with to justify the raise I already have decided to give, within the established budget?"

Inflation forces employers to provide constant pay increases for everyone, not merely for the meritorious. The resulting budgetary pressures, plus the more subtle social pressures implied in an equal-pay-for-equal-work doctrine, albeit widely justified, have helped to turn some merit raises into cost-of-living increases and so to dilute to that extent the presumed purpose of appraisals.

The halo effect referred to earlier, plus the very fact that appraisals exist, can lead to problems. Many middle managers feel they have been treated unfairly. They believe they have been passed over to make way for favored younger people and have therefore been deprived of promotions that were rightfully theirs. Further, some have been forced into early retirement. Consequently, age discrimination suits have begun to find their way into the courts, based on what is conceived to be unfair treatment.

The existence in the files of appraisals that show halo evaluations of the older manager's performance over many years does not help a company's claim that an individual was passed over because of unsatisfactory performance. A sudden downgrading of performance, just prior to passing over, doesn't help either. Does it not merely prove deliberate recent appraisal distortion to avoid the stigma of discrimination?

Other difficulties exist. For instance, one can question just how effective a formal appraisal is likely to be after it has been repeated the third or fourth time with the same participants. The nuisance of repeatedly filling out long and complicated evaluation forms, designed to put supposed science and objectivity into appraisals, doesn't really help either. Are the forms really worth the trouble?

If the purpose of an appraisal is to induce an individual to improve his performance, one may ask whether a motivated individual is not equally productive without the appraisal. One should also ask: Who is the appraiser? Is he respected by the subordinate? If he is respected and a good manager, is the formal appraisal needed, or will the subordinate already know how he is doing from communication in day-to-day supervision? If the superior hasn't let his subordinate know how he's doing, except at appraisal time, how good a manager is he, and how good therefore is the appraisal?

Evidently, the appraisal really represents the superior's justification to his own superiors of pay raises or promotions. It also serves as the basis, perhaps even justification, for the selection of people to promote to jobs administered by others than the appraisee's own boss.

There are other questions. For example, according to Earl Bark, an official of Bernard Haldane Associates, an executive counseling firm, quoted in the May 23, 1978, *Wall Street*

Journal article already referred to, many managers feel threatened by their more creative employees. A threatened manager "won't wipe out a guy's performance rating—he'll just hold him down. Most will leave before the problem comes to light." Of course, a manager who continuously does a bad job of rating subordinates, whether purposely or not, will eventually be uncovered. However, in a large company this may take a long time, and correcting it may take even longer.

How objective can appraisals be? Appraisals of an individual tend most certainly to be very subjective. Thus a 1973 survey by the American Management Association found that most executives felt advancement is based chiefly on arbitrary decisions or else on evaluations—appraisals—that are largely subjective. Because they are subjective there will tend to be inconsistencies in how different managers appraise the same individual. This showed up in a 1976 Ford Motor Company survey, according to which more than half of the salaried employees believed there was little consistency in the standards used by supervisors to rate performance.[1]

Subjectivity in appraisals is exacerbated because most companies, at least in the past, have required managers to rate subordinates on personal traits as well as on strictly job performance. It is hard to avoid bias in rating traits, and indeed some court decisions have recognized this. For example, the courts found that the appraisal system of the Cooperative Extension Service of Mississippi was used to discriminate against blacks. Much of the performance review was devoted to traits and general characteristics: leadership, attitudes, personal conduct, public acceptance, grooming, mental alertness, loyalty, and so forth.[2] Appraisal of an individual's characteristics —initiative, judgment, creativity, tact, stability, personality, attitude—generally means appraisal by unmeasured and nonuniform standards, by different managers with different per-

---

1. *Wall Street Journal*, April 29, 1977.
2. *Wall Street Journal*, May 23, 1978.

ceptions of both individuals and the importance of what they are appraising.

Even if there were no problems of consistency and the ability to measure were precise and accurate, there would still be the problems of the relative importance of different characteristics and, basically, of their validity. Just how much and to what degree are the characteristics appraised related to work performance? How valid is an appraisal based on items that are not wholly related to job accomplishment? To relate individual characteristics to performance and then to validate the correlation between the two is horrendously difficult. That is why very few companies ever even try to validate. In most companies supervisory personnel, managers, are also asked to estimate a subordinate's potential for promotion. That is totally subjective if anything is. Particularly is this so in cases where companies ask supervisors to predict how far a subordinate can rise. Doesn't this assume a supervisor really knows what it takes to be successful several levels up beyond where he himself currently is in the organization?

Performance must be measured in terms of accomplishment against objectives. The measurement of accomplishment itself is often a problem. More particularly, however, the setting of objectives in anything like quantitative terms against which accomplishment can be measured is a highly subjective procedure. Further, how does one avoid subjectivity in weighting the importance of accomplishment towards one objective compared to another, where progress towards multiple objectives varies, as it will?

In some systems of appraisal, particularly those falling in the category "management by objectives" the boss sits down with his subordinate. They negotiate, and the subordinate supposedly sets objectives for himself. This is followed three months, six months, or a year later by an evaluation, sometimes even a self-evaluation, in discussion with the boss, of performance against those objectives. Does this amount to a cat-and-mouse game? The appraiser, the cat, plays with his victim, the appraisee. In effect, the appraisee is asked to express, not what he himself believes, but rather what he guesses his boss, the appraiser, wants him to believe objectives ought to be, as well as his guess on how the superior judges his past performance.

Does this really add to human dignity? How meaningful is either the appraisal or its acceptance by the appraisee? The effectiveness of any appraisal as a tool for improving performance must rest on genuine acceptance by the appraisee of the validity of the appraisal.

Or is the appraisal, the whole formal appraisal system, merely another form of "the carrot and the stick?"

We are suggesting that formal appraisal systems are a nuisance at best and can be dangerous at worst. They can be an affront to human dignity.

The kind of appraisal a manager gives a subordinate may vary with the quality of the subordinate's performance, but it varies even more with the—

1. perceived supply of and demand for personnel able to fill the employee's job;
2. requirements of the system for the granting of predetermined pay raises;
3. ratings given by other managers to their subordinates;
4. very subjective judgments of the appraiser;
5. personal biases of the appraiser and the appraiser's perceptions of the biases of his superior and the organization;
6. conceptions or misconceptions of those who have formulated the appraisal system.

Hypotheses:

The following hypotheses relating to systematic formal appraisals are unproven, but so largely are the claims of the proponents of formal appraisal systems.

Appraisals tend to be more independent of than dependent on true performance.

Appraisals may vary inversely with performance—where a

manager either feels threatened by a creative employee, or wishes to hold onto an unusually able subordinate and therefore seeks to prevent his promotion to other duties.

Appraisals are just as likely to demotivate as to motivate— where self-appraisal either has been or still is considerably higher than is the boss's appraisal.

15

Management by Objectives Is Basic to Good Management

Reality: Management by objectives has been widely and for some time now touted as fundamental to good management. In truth, it can be meaningless or even frustrating and restrictive. Furthermore, real and declared objectives quite frequently do not coincide.

Management by objectives (MBO) refers to the utilization of formalized written objectives, which serve as the established goals an enterprise seeks to achieve. It is assumed that the existence of such objectives will improve performance. It is also assumed that the performance of individual managers can be appraised on the basis of achievement of individual goals set for those managers in the context of the overall objectives of the organization.

If objectives are stated in general terms, they represent little but pious platitudes. Perhaps they should not be more. Frequently indeed, objectives basically are really quite simple:

We want to make money.
We, management, want to survive.

When objectives are expressed in excessive detail, confusion may arise between basic objectives or goals and the means for their accomplishment. The statements may actually describe "how," the means, rather than "what," the objectives. Furthermore, MBO can lead to the neglect of opportunities that were not included in official objectives. Of course, opportunities may be seized anyway, and the objectives then revised to make them conform to the actions taken. Is such action then MBO after the fact?

Declared and real objectives don't always coincide. For instance, the real objective of a reorganization may be the ouster of a troublesome executive, or to consolidate the power of one group at the expense of another. "Improved effectiveness," or some such term, is likely to be the way in which the objective is expressed. The following represent objectives that usually are clothed in other terms:

> This advertising campaign is to promote me.
> Remember the real objective of this efficiency study—get Jones fired!

Real objectives may not be socially acceptable, or their early disclosure may be considered inadvisable. Thus a statement of objectives may be incomplete, downplaying the less acceptable and emphasizing those that seem more proper. Diversification through acquisitions may be a worthwhile company objective. The fact that particular acquisitions could also be helpful to the personal interests of one or more members of management is not stressed as another objective. Neither is the acquisition of land for the profit of a group of property owners necessarily given as an objective in some "urban redevelopment" projects paid for by the taxpayers. Management may have the objective of closing down an obsolete plant in a high-wage city as soon as a new one can be built in a low-wage area. Until the new plant is ready to operate, there is likely to be little desire to spell out the objective except as something necessary to meet needs for new market expansion.

Objectives may be kept undisclosed or deliberately vague for various other reasons. Thus a president may wish to wait for time and circumstances to develop a favorable climate on his board of directors before he discloses his proposal for an expensive entry into a new market or the sale of an unprofitable division. Objectives may be kept vague because the people writing them are unsure what they should be; management hopes future developments will bring enlightenment. Vagueness is sometimes the format of compromise. And objectives may be kept deliberately general in order not to discourage initiative and even sometimes to protect those at the top who have set up the objectives.

One is reminded of the case some years ago when a couple of fellows from one of our large corporations went to jail for meeting with the competition and setting prices, "achieving market stabilization," in violation of antitrust laws. The chief executive officer presumably had insisted that certain profit objectives be met—and maybe he felt the details did not have to be spelled out but had best be left to the initiative of subordinates. Of course, he knew nothing (or did he?) of the price fixing, which may have been about the only way the profit objectives could have been met. Anyway, the CEO did not go to jail.

Speaking of spelling out details, one retail executive a while back got fired for spelling out details—in writing. A discount house was cutting prices on merchandise bearing a high-fashion brand name. So—in line with the objective of getting rid of this problem—the manufacturer was told to stop selling to the discount house if he wanted to maintain his business with the legitimate department stores. About a year later, the department stores settled the resulting antitrust case. Six months after that, the man who tried to get the manufacturer to stop sales to the discount house was let go for being stupid enough to have written a memo spelling out the objective. The memo got subpoenaed, and it turned out to be very expensive.

The objectives of an organization, whatever they are, are not those of an abstract entity. They are subjective. They are those of the people who run that organization. For a small, privately held firm, they are those of the individuals or families who own it. For the large organization, publicly held, they are those of the managers who run it. Objectives may change with changes in control. Even when control remains the same, objectives may alter with developments in the ideas of the controlling individuals or groups.

The personality of the dominant member of top management will greatly affect an organization's objectives. For example, a man managing an organization may be interested in growth and rapid development, even at some risk, because of his temperament, because he is young, or because such growth and development will serve his own personal objectives. An older man in the dominating post who is ready to retire in a few years may have a more conservative outlook. He has an interest in conserving, with a minimum of risk, what already exists. It is his last job. He wants to feel he has left a financially sound company and, incidentally, one that will also be in a position to pay him a pension for the years ahead.

A company run by its owners may have the primary objective of maximizing profits. In enterprises controlled by non-owning managers, the profit objective will more often be steady growth rather than maximization. Other objectives include survival for the management, as well as for the firm, higher salaries for management, the satisfaction of management's ego (which may take different forms), growth and bigness for its own sake, power, prestige in the community, technical leadership, or simply a feeling of accomplishment by doing something no one else has done. Or a company's primary objective may be a higher price for its stock, which on a personal basis translates into benefits for management owning stock options. Lastly, objectives may encompass as elementary a goal as stable employment for the company's work force.

Even the occasional personal objective of a Number One, "I want to hang on until I get my retirement pension," can become, though not openly, one of the objectives by which a company or a department is guided. This personal objective is not at all unusual for older managers who have reached either the top or their level of incompetence, and for whom the job has long since been an exercise in routine.

"Never mind company objectives. I'm Number One here and my *objective is to hang on till retirement."*

If MBO is to be used effectively, objectives insofar as possible should be quantified. Objectives without specifics, preferably numbers, tend to be meaningless. One can express in numbers goals such as output, costs per unit, earnings per share, total sales, rate of growth of sales, share of market, and return on investment. Objectives involving output and costs per unit of output should also include measures for quality. It is more difficult to express in numbers such abstract goals as technical excellence, community leadership, or good citizenship. Some specifics and numbers can, however, be formulated for these, even though the measures used and the figures may be subjective and far from unbiased.

More immediate objectives sometimes are set by working backwards from more distant goals. What one wants to accomplish in five years may be broken up into segments to be accomplished in year one, then year two, and so forth.

If the level of performance set as an objective is too high, those who are to perform may well give up right from the start. They are defeated by a feeling of frustration, on the supposition that there is no point in knocking themselves out to achieve what is just not achievable. MBO can be frustrating.

If objectives are set too low, lower than can be readily achieved, the full potential for achievement will not be reached. Furthermore, in this situation truly achievement-oriented managers are likely to be frustrated by the realization that management is not pushing as hard for achievement as it should.

Objectives should remain somewhat flexible and realistic. They need to be reviewed at least annually, or more often as circumstances and perceptions change.

If overall objectives for an organization are set, then their achievement also requires the setting of objectives for units within the organization—subsidiaries, divisions, branches, and departments. However, the establishment of objectives in organizational subunits can lead to internal company conflict. Assume a manufacturing department's objective is to keep costs per unit produced below a given figure. Assume that at the same time the marketing department's objective is to increase sales volume by a specific percentage. To create more interest and sales, the marketing group wishes to diversify the product's colors, styles, and design variations. To keep costs per unit down, the manufacturing department wishes to limit product variations.

The conflict between the two objectives could be eliminated if the objective set for the manufacturing costs per unit were based on a formula that fairly took into account the mix of color, style, and design variations, and if the sales department's objectives were expressed in terms of contribution to profit and overhead. Such formulas would allow decision making on the basis of the total effect—of product variations on sales volumes, of selling prices, and of manufacturing, inventory, servicing, and other costs. The resulting objectives would be fair to both managers and also provide maximum benefit to the company.

To meet an objective of lowered cost, the group that maintains a dairy's delivery fleet may wish to invest a given number of dollars in repair facilities for work it now contracts out. To meet a sales objective, the marketing department may want to use the same dollars for an augmented advertising campaign. The resolution of this conflict lies with top management, which must judge priorities and then make the requisite allocations.

Another type of conflict in objectives within an organization is illustrated by the chamber of commerce that pushes for lower taxes and, at the same time, for a civic auditorium that will require major tax revenue funding. Or the CEO whose main objectives for the coming year are cutting administrative expenses while at the same time completing new enlarged offices to replace more-than-adequate existing facilities.

Those espousing MBO have assumed that, if objectives— expectations as to performance—are specified, improved performance will result. If motivation is adequate this is likely to be true, in view of our hypothesis on performance and expectations. *Performance is directly related to the level of expectations and desire*—provided the expectations are within the limits of what physically and otherwise can be accomplished, and the desire is sufficient to bring out the required effort.[1]

Assuming objectives are feasible, the key is motivation. On

---

1. See chapter 12.

that score there are some reservations to keep in mind about MBO.

Are not general objectives likely to be known, or to be developed by achievement-oriented managers, whether or not a specific, detailed listing of objectives is formally spelled out? Will those managers who are achievement oriented likely be so in any case, whether or not an MBO program is implemented? How much will a formal MBO program really add to motivation and effectiveness? Or will the additional time and paperwork required serve as a medium of frustration and wasted effort?

Will those managers who are less achievement oriented be motivated by a formalized, detailed MBO program? Possibly! But will this be merely a temporary initial motivation that dies out, either after the first enthusiasm or after a raise, or else after the initially watchful eye of the superior has been diverted from MBO to other areas needing attention?

In theory, participants, including lower and middle management, are supposed to be involved in setting their own objectives and therefore should be motivated to achieve those objectives set by themselves. But these same managers must set their subunit objectives within the context of top-management objectives. Do they, therefore, really have that much influence over their objectives? In effect, in practice, is the situation much different from that of the boss addressing his subordinates:

> Well, those are my ideas for your objectives in the next year. A little low, but better that than too high. Don't you think so? Now—let's hear your ideas.

Often an MBO program is used as a whip. This may lead to results, but will they ultimately be greater than with other whip-type programs?

MBO may be used as a tool for appraising managers. This is based on the supposition that results can be measured against objectives, providing a fair gauge of performance. Such measurement does not, however, avoid the question of whether objectives are set high or low compared to what realistically can be achieved. Nor does it avoid questions of unanticipated good or bad luck, and the evaluation of the effect of luck on performance.

In considering formal MBO programs it must be remembered that, within an organization, individual departments or groups will have their own informal objectives. Included in these may well be objectives inconsistent with those of top management. People do learn to play games. If objectives call for certain numbers, somehow those numbers show up, though their real meaning may not correspond at all to what had been intended.

Speaking of games—MBO programs can have other undesirable effects. Cost-reduction programs can be met by deferring needed maintenance. Sales volume can be pushed up by marketing easily sold, low-profit items or by cutting prices —never mind later problems and retaliation by the competition.

Too much emphasis on reaching agreed-upon goals can lead to the sacrifice of everything else in the attempt to reach them. Sticking rigidly to established objectives when they have become inappropriate can lead to problems.

Putting MBO to work means, not only setting overall objectives for an organization, but within their context detailing the objectives of all the parts and groups within the organization. This requires work—the delicate balance of setting objectives, from above, with or without initial real or supposed participation from the bottom. It also presupposes an ability to monitor and to appraise performance in the light of the objectives set. Often the considerable extra work of formalizing objectives, the discussions with subordinates and by them in turn with their subordinates, the paperwork, and the myriad details of coordination and all the rest that follows simply are not worth the trouble.

It is likely that MBO programs, if they are not overdone,

are best utilized at upper management levels. Reservations as to MBO's effectiveness are greatest in respect to lower management echelons, but they are also great where objectives are set forth in excessive detail and the pursuit of that detail is treated too seriously.

In summary, management by objectives, the aggressive spelling out and pursuit of objectives in detail, is likely to divert effort from the attainment of basic goals to concentration on specific means. It tends to discourage flexibility and the exploitation of opportunities not included in the official objectives. Additionally, it encourages the devotion of time and effort to the development of a "party line" along with its accompanying paperwork and bureaucracy. Lastly, people play games with numbers when it comes to meeting objectives.

Hypothesis:

The more aggressively an organization pursues management by objectives, the less likely is it to achieve its goals.

16

Good Planning Is Based on Objective Forecasts, Analyses, and Rational Choices among Alternatives

Reality: Yes, planning is supposed to be based on objective forecasts, estimates now of what is likely to happen in the future, but such estimates are not objective. They are subjective. Further, planning may not actually be based on forecasts; rather, forecasts are likely to be shaped by the planning. That is, the planning comes first, and the forecast follows.

Planning is a process of mapping out action so as either to change favorably what is believed will otherwise happen, or to take the maximum advantage of opportunities forecast for the future. Rational choices among alternatives are what planning should be all about. However, planning is based on forecasts, and these are very much swayed by expectations, which in turn are influenced by many other factors. Expectations include those related to local, U.S., and international economic and business conditions, inflation rates, and the political, regulatory, and legal climate. Other extraneous factors include the weather, which, through its effect on crops influences economics, and politics. Also to be considered are population growth; prices; the availability of capital, materials, energy, labor, and talent; the outlook for an industry and its customers; and the

strength, strategy, and thrust of competition. Not to be overlooked are developments in technology that may affect the
market demand for what a company sells and perhaps even
the very nature of a firm's product.

The elements listed above obviously are mostly external
to an enterprise and generally beyond its control. However,
internal factors, those having to do with management, technology and know-how, personnel, physical facilities, and availability of capital must also be estimated for the coming
year(s), if planning is to be successful.

We firmly believe that expectations as to both external and
internal factors cannot be objective. In truth, they are highly
subjective and are influenced largely by three elements.

Probably the most important is history. Expectations for
the future are largely arrived at by extrapolating from the past,
and in the absence of other, firmer guidelines, this is as it
should be. Extrapolation by its very nature is subjective.

A second element is the very natural human desire to believe what one wants to believe. One important factor is generally a sense of optimism. Also included are biases and desires
entertained by management and by technicians and other personnel who provide information and interpretations to management. Technicians and other subordinates sometimes find
it wise, whether consciously or not, to reflect in their argu-
ments and calculations or assessments what they think the boss
believes or what they think he really wants to hear. This is a
very human tendency and should not be overlooked.

Finally, of some considerable importance, though also influenced by history and wishful thinking, are the opinions of
others outside the organization, expressed through personal
contacts, meetings, and the public media.

Planning is supposed to be based on forecasts, but frequently
the forecast is based on the planning. Any good manager is
aware of the occasional adjustment of forecasts of costs, markets, and pricing to make a pet project come out with the rate
of return on investment required to receive approval of the

chief executive officer and the company's board of directors. And in more than one organization, perception of what the boss wants is of considerable importance in shaping supposedly objective reports by internal researchers, analysts, and managers. Even outside research people and consultants can at times be pressured into coming up with preset answers—for example, on the feasibility of a petrochemical plant or the desirability of moving a company's headquarters to where a new president wishes to live. It is common observation that management's decisions, not always but frequently, are made before the internal staff or outside research people and consultants begin planning studies and analyses of alternative choices. The outsider is often hired for the express purpose of justifying what has already been decided, and he very often knows it. This is done partly so that the decision maker personally can feel more secure and reassured about the wisdom of his own decision, and partly to point to the outside study as justification and authority should the decision later be questioned by board members asked to approve expenditures or by stockholders or the public. All of this may not be rational, but it exists.

In planning, it is well to remember that what is intellectually most desirable may not necessarily be the best among alternative goals or courses of action. The practical realities of organizational biases, personalities, strengths of competing departments, and so on sometimes have a greater impact than do detailed analyses or reason alone. The best planning may not be based solely on rationality. In fact, rationality in planning may result in a paradox.

Suppose, for example, a company prepares and implements plans to expand the capacity of its plant in order to take advantage of an anticipated increase in demand and coincidentally to carve out a larger market share. Competitors, also aware of the increased demand, will more than likely make similar plans or, at the very least, will respond with other actions of their own. The industry may find itself having over-capacity, with no single company gaining a greater market share. In fact, with the increased capacity built by current and perhaps new competitors who have also planned for the increased demand, an individual firm may find it has an even smaller sales volume than before, but greater overhead costs. This is especially so if anticipated increases in total market demand do not fully materialize.

Planning cannot possibly foresee all that actually can happen in the future, and thus no plan can be followed logically, or for that matter should be followed precisely. Plans often must be disregarded or altered if they are not to be restrictive, or if one is to take advantage of unforeseen opportunities.

Changes in top management or in the outlook of existing management can completely alter an organization's objective and viewpoint and so make previous plans obsolete. Planning will be heavily influenced by what management decides are its goals and priorities, and by its interpretation of what is needed to meet those goals and priorities.

No one set of plans is right for an organization. Each of a number of alternatives can succeed or fail for any one firm at any one time and under any one set of circumstances.

Luck too has a part to play. It often determines whether an action is considered brilliant or stupid.

Management may deliberately plan for less than it believes can be achieved. It's easier to meet or exceed modest objectives than to reach for more ambitious goals calling for a greater effort and perhaps carrying a greater risk of failure. Being conservative may be the better part of wisdom. Even success, where ambitious goals have been established, may merely set an unwelcome precedent, requiring matching or even more effort and risk in the future.

On the other hand management and those responsible for feeding it information may be optimists by nature. They may therefore plan "high." Such planning may also be deliberate. It does make everyone, even sometimes the stock market, optimistic about a company. Explanations for subsequent below-plan performance can be worked out later—after, for example, a desired upsurge in the price of a stock, or after competition has been scared out of proceeding with a parallel plant expansion.

Planning should not be judged by how closely results conform with what was planned, that is, the accuracy of prediction. The fact that results closely approximated plans does not necessarily mean an enterprise planned well. It could merely mean that the planning called for less-than-optimum performance. No brilliance would be required to meet such goals, even with unforeseen difficulties and an unwillingness to push innovative ideas or to take business risks.

The more ably aggressive the management, the more likely is it to deviate from plans, and by a greater degree, in terms of either exceeding or falling short of planned performance.

Good planning means plans are likely not to be met. Plans are most likely to be met when planning is poor.

Planning is intended to guide action decisions that must be made today which will affect tomorrow. Planning for decisions affecting the future that need not be made until tomorrow had best be done tomorrow, after the enterprise has that much more information and can do that much less guessing about the factors that will affect the future. A little fuzziness in planning where clarification can await tomorrow may therefore be advantageous, rather than otherwise.

As with objectives, a little vagueness in planning may also be desirable in order to avoid confrontation between two separate interest groups in an organization: time and circumstances may develop the appropriate resolution of potential conflicts.

Planning's greatest contribution to an enterprise is not the plan, but the process of forcing a review and thinking-through of objectives and programs. Therefore, the actual planning may be more important than the plan.

Planning is intended to focus on major objectives, providing a frame of reference to help top management make commitments more rapidly and effectively, and to achieve coordination and teamwork throughout the organization. Planning provides a mechanism for increasing sensitivity to the changes, problems, and opportunities that can affect the organization's future. Blueprinting the future should not be so restrictive as to prevent seizing unforeseen opportunities merely because they weren't planned.

Once in a while planning has a cosmetic purpose. It may be intended to encourage prospective lenders and sources of capital—banks, insurance companies, or other investors—to believe in the future of the company and the ability of its management.

Sometimes it's intended to reassure management itself that it is modern, up-to-date in its techniques and modes of conducting an enterprise. Sometimes, too, planning for a wonderful future eases the pain of facing a discouraging present.

Hypotheses:

The plan tends to come first; the forecast on which a plan is to be based *tends to follow*—not the reverse.

The more one strives for strict rationality in planning, the poorer is likely to be the plan. Among alternatives, that which is best may not be that which is most rational.

The better the planning, the more likely it is that results will not conform to what has been planned. Plans and performance will most easily coincide when an enterprise deliberately plans for underachievement, that is to say, when planning is poor.

The process of planning is more important than the plan.

17

A Budget for an Organization Is an Intellectually Logical Plan; It Curtails Waste and Unnecessary Expenditures

Reality: Quite to the contrary, a budget inherently cannot be strictly logical. Not only that, it can and often does encourage waste and unnecessary expenditures.

There are two types of budgets, operating and capital. Here we shall concern ourselves only with operating budgets. An operating budget is a short-term plan, generally for one year, commonly broken down by quarter, often by months, that is intended to provide a blueprint for the operation of the company in that year.

A budget serves as a forecast of expected revenue, expenses, and profit or loss. It also serves as a means for estimating how much cash will be needed and how much will be available. If borrowing will be needed to meet peak demands, a budget provides the basis for making necessary borrowing arrangements.

A budget also serves as a medium for the allocation of an organization's resources. The allocation ought to be rational. This means, for example, that the final dollar provided Department A ought to yield as much as the final dollar provided Department B. The addition to or loss prevented in net worth by the expenditure of the last dollar should be equal for both departments. If the final dollar allocated Department A yields less than the final dollar provided Department B, then the organization would be better off to switch that dollar from A to B. This is true for other departments, for all subunits, and for that matter for all functions of an organization. Of course, the influence of interrelationships must be considered insofar as amounts allocated to A may affect the output, costs, or sales of B, C, or D.

Practically, it is impossible to estimate even approximately the value received for each extra dollar spent in all the various ways that dollar can be spent. That alone means a budget inherently cannot be totally logical. Estimating is further complicated by errors in forecasting economic and business conditions and by the relative values to be placed on longer-run as against short-run returns.

A budget is intended to control expenditures, to keep costs in line with what is needed, and with the anticipated revenues to produce a given profit or to limit an expected loss, short run, in accord with objectives. Quite consciously, it is supposed to be mindful also of long-run objectives and such needs as there may be to spend money currently to achieve those objectives later on. Because it is a short-term plan, generally for one year, it does emphasize the priority of short-run objectives, often to the detriment of longer-run considerations. Obviously, this may not be the best logically for an organization, but a budget works that way. It produces a short-term priority.

Both in the formulation of a budget and its implementation, rationality is destroyed by the emphasis on short-run operations and the pressure brought to bear on managers to meet the budget. If illogical actions sometimes follow, they are to be expected.

Thus, for example, if it is necessary to meet budgetary limits, costs can be cut by curtailing maintenance, though this hurts the longer run. So also cuts can be made in advertising and promotion outlays, even if this means undercutting the organization's long-run market share. The pressure of meeting short-run goals may lead to cutting back funds for training and development, which means that "people building" for the future will suffer, another illogical action. This all adds up to waste for the years ahead, particularly for organizations that, because of their financial strength, can afford to and should take the wiser, long-term approach, not a series of short-term views.

Another problem interferes with what budgeting is supposed to accomplish. In the United States as well as in Russia, managers learn to provide in all kinds of ways the "figures" called for by a budget, ways that mislead and are only later, maybe, uncovered. For example, a lot can be done with the method by which inventory is valued. The usual write-down of obsolete inventory can be delayed until it can be handled more conveniently, in another year's budget. Costs of ordinary equipment repairs can be turned into costs for "rebuilt" equipment that can be capitalized, with expenditures written off over several years instead of all in the current budget. A number of other things can be done to distort data into conformance with budget requirements. In one case known to the authors, even advertising costs were capitalized. All this hardly helps make the budget's implementation an exercise in total logic.

Similarly, the pressures of budgetary limits may prevent the sensible exploitation of an unexpected opportunity. For example, to promote an existing product for a newly discovered use may mean only a limited increase in sales for the current year but a large increase in promotion and selling costs in the same year—well above what the budget allowed for. In most cases, unfortunately, the anticipated increase in profit in later years is of less pressing concern than is the need to meet a current year's budget. Again, this is not really logical.

The impossibility of a completely intelligent allocation of an organization's resources is underscored by the fact that any budget represents a compromise. It is a compromise based on history, the economic and political climate in which the organization operates, the desires and fears of the organization's top management, and the relative strength and negotiating skill of those who participate in the formulation of a budget. Of course, in all budgeting what the competition does is also relevant.

Some years ago, the research vice-president of a large oil company confessed that he never had any difficulty in getting his budget requests approved by the chief executive officer and the board of directors. Instead of presenting a detailed recitation of the whys and wherefores of his requests, he merely pointed out how many dollars each of the other leading oil companies were spending on research. The response was predictable—not "Why do we need to spend so much?" but rather, "Are you sure we're spending enough?" Comparisons with the competition, incidentally, do have a certain rationale.

It is well known, of course, that a budget is the end product of a negotiating process. One aspect of this is the frequency with which, at budget-formulation time, a department manager will overestimate expected expenditures for the coming year. He assumes he will be cut back. The company's controller, on the other hand, will try more often than not to reduce the estimates to a figure less than is realistically required. He knows he can then compromise upward. The result is a game, a negotiating game.

To the department manager the questions are: How much will the controller or his staff cut me down? Therefore, how much must I add to what I really need? How much can I get by with? The controller and his staff wonder: How much have the figures been puffed up? How much must I cut? Both the department manager and the controller have a stake in the game. The manager wants to be sure he gets enough money to run his department and maybe to look good, even to show a little saving at the end of the budget year. The controller wants to show on the record that he has done his job: "See how much money I have saved the company by forcing these fellows to learn how to operate with less?"

Which department manager is going to look better at the

end of the year—the fellow who is completely honest in submitting a budget he thinks he can live with, including an allowance for cost reductions he believes he can make, or the fellow who inflates his estimate of needs and, at the very least, withholds information on the cost cutting he could and probably will implement in his department?

Budgets tend to perpetuate the status quo because of both current negotiating strength and history. Funds are generally allocated in proportion to the existing strength of products, product lines, divisions, and branches rather than rationally in proportion to their potential for profit. An existing product line may face a drastic decline in popularity in the coming years. It may be logical, therefore, to allocate heavily to research and development and to organize a sales effort for newer lines of products that will take the place of the old. Instead, the human tendency is to fight the tide, to try to shore up the old. Funds and effort are allocated more strongly and far longer to the old, less strongly and later to the new, than sound action would dictate.

A budget encourages waste and unnecessary expenditures. How? By encouraging full spending of one's budget, once moneys have been allocated. Thus it has been common for government agencies to make sure that all budgeted funds are spent by the end of each fiscal year. There is a virtual rush as the end of a budget year approaches to make sure all unexpended moneys are spent. The rush is motivated by fear that, if less than the appropriated funds is used, future budgeted amounts will be cut. This philosophy holds particularly true in the public sector, but even in profit-making organizations it is important not to underspend.

To give a small example, a friend recently insisted that his secretary list a new desk and some other office funiture in the departmental budget requests for the coming year. The furniture wasn't really needed. However, it had been customary to regularly include a furniture allowance of about $1,500 in the annual budget. If the item were omitted in the coming year, to reinstate it when the furniture actually was needed would produce a hassle. But no one would question a continuation.

The tendency to make sure allocated funds are spent is often carried to an even greater extreme by charitable, educational, and cultural organizations such as operas, ballets, and the arts in general. As the controller of a large private university once explained to one of the authors, "A university should always spend more than is available. If it balances its budget, it's never going to expand its programs. You need to be in the red, with a large deficit to be made up, if you plan to cry effectively to your alumni and friends for help. Why should anyone donate if your budget is in the black, that is, if you apparently don't need help?"[1]

A budget tends to be looked on as an expense-control medium. While we admit this function is useful, it often de-emphasizes the use of a budget as a tool for allocating the investment of resources in profit-making activities.

A budget serves as a whip for exerting pressure on managers to do all sorts of unpleasant things to people and at the same time makes it easy for managers to excuse themselves from the actions they take. A budget can be blamed as a reason for firing people. Managers find it easy to point to the detested budget as justification for refusing a raise. How many times has one heard, "I really went to bat for you, but—it's the damned budget."

The budget is especially used as a cost-cutting tool when profits are down. Over-budget cost deviations can be and are tolerated when profits are up. They are rigidly policed with corrective action when profits are down.

We believe a budget may serve to unify lower and middle management against top management. To a degree a budget takes away the right of the manager of a subsidiary, division, branch, or department to run his own show, and managers often perceive this. For this reason alone it is frequently re-

---

1. See chapter 3.

sented. The resentment often shows, sometimes in indirect ways—for example, passive resistance.

A budget definitely contributes to disharmony in an organization. Too often the budget process makes it clear that more money given to Departments B, C, and D means less money for Department A. The objective then of the manager of Department A is to fight for his own piece of the total, and not to concern himself with an overall company view of how much Departments B, C, and D need.

It is possible, for example, that a budget would encourage Department A to avoid spending a given number of dollars to reduce variability in the dimensions of a part used in a company's products—an improvement that would reduce costs in Departments B, C, and D by several times that many dollars. A's performance is measured by its expenses and not by cost reduction achieved elsewhere in the organization. Thus, a budget can actively hurt as well as help in producing profit.

There are also situations where Department A might learn to make certain savings by doing something differently. Department B would also save if it would do the same. However, the manager of Department A might be reluctant to reveal to his superiors more than he needs to about the role of improved methods for fear of focusing undue attention on himself, thus initiating pressures for still further economies. Furthermore, it is more than likely that colleagues might not altogether appreciate ensuing pressures on themselves to follow suit with improved performances. Not everybody loves a rate buster, whether he be a blue-collar worker, a white-collar clerk who widely outproduces the normal work standards, or an eager-beaver manager who shows up mediocrity of performance in other managers.

If a manager does not meet his budget, he is under pressure to place the blame elsewhere. Who hasn't heard the excuses: If only the sales department had been less anxious to sell non-standard designs or colors, manufacturing cost would not have been as high. If only engineering had not insisted on unrealistic specifications, the cost of purchasing parts could have been more reasonable. If only manufacturing had not missed getting orders out on time, several good customers would not have been lost. Each manager, with the pressure of the budget trained on him, looks out for himself. Team work suffers.

A budget pits staff, particularly the controller's staff, against line. The situation encourages antagonistic roles. The controller wins brownie points if he can jump on items for which expenditures exceed budgeted amounts. He can demand corrective action on such over-budget expenditures by pointing them out to his senior management, which then turns to the line managers involved. The controller has justified his position. He has been able to save the company substantial sums of money in his role as budget watchdog, though he may have antagonized line management in the process.

It is just as important to know why less money than budgeted is spent as to know why more is spent. Underspending may mean undermaintenance—cheap now, expensive later. Or it could mean improved methods, and in this case initial improvements made may point the way to still further improvements, applicable perhaps also to nonimproved areas in the organization.

Despite its drawbacks a budget is a useful tool. The very process of making up a budget forces a thinking-through of objectives and operations. This process may be a budget's most important function.

A budget provides a measure of performance: a control mechanism setting profit goals and an operational blueprint by which a subsidiary can be measured. It thus permits a degree of decentralization. In other words, each unit can be allowed to run itself, so long as overall budgeting guideposts exist to provide top management with an early warning system on any forthcoming difficulties. The effectiveness of the allocation of a company's funds is reflected in the profitability of the different segments of the organization to which allocations have been made. In this context budgeting makes more difficult the task of a subordinate who for his own reasons may wish to bury unprofitable operations by combining their figures with those of more profitable areas.

A budget includes a forecast of income and expenses. Forecasts are subject to error, however. The use of a fixed budget, based on forecasts, for expenditures which will vary with actual sales and output, therefore is not completely realistic. Perverse as it may seem, the fixed budget does have one advantage for this very reason. It forces an organization to forecast as well as possible. This is basic to good planning. Good forecasting provides a basis for estimating exactly how much cash will be needed and when. It provides specific goals.

However, an alternative is a variable budget that provides financial guidelines based on a range of likely sales. This furnishes flexibility for the allocation of expenditures under various conditions; the budget changes with the actual volume of business. Fluctuations in price and mix of product sold, and in costs of materials, labor, and services purchased, can be allowed for by budget modification approaches. Such fluctuations are commonly taken into account in explanations of why deviations from budget have occurred.

In its simplest form, variable budgeting is based on the assumption that some costs are fixed regardless of unit volume, and others vary directly in proportion to that volume. The breakdown of costs into fixed and variable is reflected in breakeven charts that can at times help top management project the effects on profit of changes in volume and costs. As a result, management can determine how much to emphasize increasing volume or decreasing costs, to reach given profit goals.

Costs that vary don't always change directly in proportion to volume. Doubling volume may not double material costs. They may more than double because of rejects produced by inexperienced people added to the production line. On the other hand, they may less than double because the increased amounts of materials or components purchased for the additional output result in a lower unit cost. The cost of direct labor and services similarly may not vary directly in proportion to volume of output.

The reasonableness of cost estimates for either fixed or variable budgets can be checked by the use of relatively simple statistical quartile, hysteresis, or other analyses. Learning curve calculations are at times also appropriate.

Fixed and variable budgets can be used together to supplement each other.

A manager can control some costs. However, he cannot control others, such as depreciation charges on equipment, rental costs, and corporate overhead costs allocated to his department. Thus a manager should only be held responsible for the costs he can control. Budgets should reflect this viewpoint.

Interference with a manager's control of his departmental costs by excessive monitoring can be counterproductive. For example, midway into a budget year a department head may find it desirable to shift expenditures from one category to another. Detailed questioning, explanation, requestioning, and time-consuming defense for the shifting can be costly in effort, money, and morale, with little gained. If monitoring is excessive a manager may find it simpler to switch funds within his department by mislabeling expenditures or changing definitions of budgeted categories. He can get away with this if the financial people do not catch it or choose to look the other way.

A budget to a degree reflects the individuality of top management. This personality is reflected in the amounts allocated to advertising, to research and development, and to personnel and management training.

Hypotheses:

A budget inherently cannot be intellectually logical. Even were that theoretically possible, the budget, the end product of a negotiating process amongst conflicting interests within an organization, would be hostage to the desires and the relative strength and skill of the negotiators. It generally overemphasizes the spending controls function to the detriment of the investment function in the allocation of an organization's resources. At the same time budgets can and do encourage waste and unnecessary spending. A budget provides both pressure and a rationalization for firing people and doing other nasty things, while shifting the blame from the doer to an impersonal document.

Budgets overprotect the status quo. They discourage change and thus innovation, entrepreneurship, and increased productivity. This arises from the tendency to allocate funds in proportion to the existing rather than the potential strength of products, product lines, divisions, branches, and so forth; and from the pressures a budget creates for priority of short-run over longer-range goals.

The greater the detail in a budget, the greater is likely to be waste and unnecessary expenditure. The larger the number of specific items budgeted, the greater is the number of items likely to be allocated more money than necessary, and the greater is the conscious or subconscious temptation to avoid future budget curtailment for those items by making sure the full amounts allocated to them are spent. Where detail is less and expenditures are allocated only by broad category, there is more freedom to shift moneys around in accordance with need. Moreover, detail does require additional paperwork and other administrative costs, thereby contributing to waste.

18
Overhead Is a Fixed Expense

Reality: In many ways overhead is actually a variable cost.

It is generally believed that overhead, what is sometimes called general and administrative expense, G & A, is a fixed cost, and as such varies little with the volume of a company's sales. Actually, overhead over the long run is not fixed but takes on the characteristics of a variable expense, one that varies as a company's volume of business changes.

A few years ago, figures on G & A and on sales volume were reviewed for a random sampling of large corporations. That review showed that over five- and ten-year periods, G & A increased for the companies studied generally in proportion to the increases in the volume of business. Although the correlation was imperfect, it was definite. Yet, the sampling was limited and, therefore, not completely conclusive. The results, unpublished, plus some other evidence, along with general observation over the years of how organizations operate, tend to confirm a suspicion. Even in the short run, overhead as measured by G & A tends to conform to a traditional or expected percentage of a company's sales volume. It is a variable, not a fixed expense.

Logic reinforces the limited evidence and the hunch. If
volume increases, and generally therefore profits, management's mood is expansive. While theoretically G & A need not
increase, certainly not in proportion to the increase in volume,
the tendency is to note that the G & A percentage to sales is
below normal. Control standards, therefore, tend to be re-
laxed. Old office furniture and equipment is replaced and
added to. A new secretary is hired here and there. It is discovered that a new building and additional office space are
needed. A corporate plane becomes a necessity. Another vice-
president is added. Salaries and bonuses go up. Training and
development programs are expanded. In short, G & A expense

"There goes my raise and your job."

is rectified. It is brought up to the standard, the expected percentage of sales volume.

Let sales and profits drop, and the axe is out. It suddenly becomes possible to curtail training and development. Duties are consolidated, and a vice-president is dropped. Secretaries are let go. Excess office space is sold off or leased out. The airplane is no longer needed. Bonuses are not as generous. If matters get really bad, salaries might even be cut. At any rate, it doesn't take long, whether with existing or with new management, to get G & A's percentage of volume back down to where it should be, the traditional figure.

It is recognized that, to a degree, the statements above contradict Parkinson's Law. That law implies that bureaucracy, overhead, will continue to grow year after year, regardless of what happens to volume. However, Parkinson's examples were based on government operations and bureaucracy. The law may not apply as fully where · organizations are faced with practical money limitations that prevent its free exercise.

Hypothesis:

The percentage of revenue that an organization allocates to overhead is governed by tradition. Overhead tends to be a constant percentage of revenue and as such it is a variable rather than a fixed expense.

19

Research and Development Is Generally a Good Investment

Reality: We disagree. Research and development devoted to really original work, and not merely to the refinement of what already exists, is in fact a poor investment. It represents a high-risk expenditure, most of which will not be fruitful. Only a few projects that represent truly original work will lead directly or indirectly to successful and economically feasible results, to useful inventions, and to increased productivity.

If a great many projects are undertaken, the odds favor the success of at least a few, which will more than pay for the failures. Hence, for the country as a whole, investment in new ideas, in R & D, is worthwhile. For any one industry where R & D, over a sustained period of time, is jointly and adequately supported on a large number of projects by all major companies in that industry, it is likely to be rewarding. For any one company, however, the investment risk in original work is staggeringly high. This is most definitely so in mature industries and may be so in certain still-developing areas. R & D is essential in the young, technological and fast-growing sectors of the economy. But except in these sectors, it is not likely to be as good an investment as would be a program of new acquisitions, additional marketing efforts, organization building, or investing in real estate.

Some years ago a private study of twenty-seven electronics firms was undertaken. The study compared publicly available figures on the percentage growth in sales with expenditures for R & D made three, four, five and six years earlier. Although the electronics industry is particularly oriented to spending for the new, and its spectacular growth has commonly been attributed, rightly we believe, to a willingness to spend for such effort, the study revealed that even in this industry there was no clear correlation between the rate of growth and the percentage of sales spent on R & D. Growth seemingly depended more on other factors—sales effort, management talent, entrepreneurial aggressiveness, financial abilities, acquisitions, luck, or whatnot.

These results were difficult to believe. In all honesty, some of the published data on the amounts spent for what was termed R & D could have been misleading. Errors in definition could have occurred. The study did not prove that R & D was unimportant. It may have been most important. Nevertheless, its effectiveness in producing growth was obviously greatly influenced by other factors.

A few years ago, a large, diversified machinery manufacturer reviewed its sales growth and profits and compared the results of acquisitions with those of R & D. Much had been spent on both. Growth and returns were greater from acquisitions than from the in-house effort. In other words, research and development is pioneering, and that's expensive.

Private industry has recognized the risks incurred by the individual enterprise in spending on the search for the new. It is not convinced of the worth of such spending, as is evidenced by the fact that for many years the dollars spent on private research and development have not kept pace with the gross national product. Even in an absolute sense, the manpower devoted to R & D is believed to be no more and perhaps less today than it was ten years ago. Further, over three-fourths of the expenditures labeled R & D have supported the refinement of that which already exists rather than the search for something really new.

According to a National Science Foundation survey made in 1974, about 3.5 percent of industrial research funds was spent on basic science, in other words, on the search for new knowledge without concern for specific applications. Another 20 percent was spent on applied science projects not directly tied to specific products or processes, and the balance, fully 76.5 percent, was spent on development work.[1] According to a May, 1978, White House statement, "In recent years, private sector research and development has concentrated on low-risk, short-term projects directed at improving existing products. Emphasis on the longer-term research that could lead to new products and processes has decreased."[2]

Even government spending on R & D has not emphasized the longer-term research that could lead to the really new. According to one estimate, basic research accounts for only 9.7 percent of the cost of government-sponsored defense and space work and 27 percent in other government-sponsored work.[3]

Mature businesses, from steel in heavy industry to department stores in the service industry, spend very little on R & D relative to their sales. Our steel industry is certainly noncompetitive in the world market. The failure to invest in R & D has been a factor. Of major innovations in the industry in recent years, four came from Europe, seven from independent inventors, and none from the American steel industry

One of the authors remembers a comment made in 1975

1. "Where Private Industry Puts Its Research Money," *Business Week*, June 28, 1976, pp. 62 ff.
2. *Wall Street Journal*, September 14, 1978, p. 8.
3. "New Ways to Bring Technology to the Marketplace," *Technology Review*, March/April 1977, pp. 27 ff.

by an American contracting engineer who was supervising, in
Ireland, the installation of cotton-gin machinery made in
Czechoslovakia. When asked why Czechoslovakian machinery,
the engineer smiled and said, "It's much cheaper, it's far more
reliable, and it's twice as quick as anything we have been able
to develop in the United States."

Such money as a business enterprise spends for R & D is
often determined by either tradition or what the competition
does.[4] Spending based on comparison with the competition
reflects defensive thinking rather than an aggressive belief in
the merits of such expenditures. The tendency is to assume that,
if a company spends approximately the same as does its competition and results are about as fruitful, then on the whole
the company has bought an insurance policy against unpleasant
surprises. The spending keeps a company in touch with what
does and might develop in technology, and therefore it won't
be caught unawares by anything new. It's part of the price of
retaining a firm's position in its industry, and the competitor
pays the same price.

Spending on the high-risk new rather than the lower-risk refinement, real or cosmetic, of the old has been discouraged by a
number of things. The cost of research and development is
growing. The time span between the initiation of R & D and
success in the marketplace is increasing. The probability of
failure is high. There are alternative investments.

Management too is a problem. Its increasing professionalism
means an increasing tendency to avoid undue risk. If a satisfactory return can be obtained with other investments, why
put a company's money into R & D, which could and often
does produce continuing and sometimes considerable drain on
funds with highly uncertain results. It is the entrepreneur, not
the professional manager, who is most willing to gamble.

From a manager's point of view it may be cheaper to let the
other fellow take the risks. If he comes up with something, in-

---

4. See chapter 17.

tensive copying can be relatively cheap. It avoids false starts and indicates where to concentrate development dollars. Of course, a firm doesn't have to copy directly. It can research and design "around" a successful innovation. Further, an invention can be licensed or an inventor hired away. When litigation results a deal can always be attempted.

Research and development is further discouraged by the emphasis professional management places on the short run—the result of budgeting practices, the use of discounted cash-flow analyses, and the penchant for measuring performance by return on investment.

The general adoption of discounted cash-flow analyses[5] and return on investment for judging results, along with its effect on executive bonuses,[6] poses a distinct problem. Investment for the long-run future gets heavily discounted when compared with that which will yield results right away. R & D suffers accordingly. It takes a long time for innovation to travel from idea to new product or process. Even longer is required to generate sufficient sales volume or utilization for profitability.

A study[7] of ten of the major innovations developed in the period 1933 to 1966 shows a time lapse between year of first conception and year of first realization ranging from six years for the videotape recorder to thirty-two years for the heart pacemaker (see Table 19.1).

It requires fantastic profitability to justify the long-run investment that new inventions require when the discounted cash-flow yardstick is applied to them. How many able managements, knowledgeable and sophisticated by today's standards, would have invested the necessary funds to research and to develop the really major innovations of the twentieth century?

---

5. See discussion in chapter 1.
6. "Avoiding Risks," *Wall Street Journal,* June 10, 1977, pp. 1, 25.
7. Samuel Globe, Girard W. Levy, and Charles M. Schwartz, Battelle's Columbus Laboratories, "Key Factors and Events in the Innovation Process," *Research Management,* July 1973, pp. 8–15.

Table 19.1

Duration of the Innovative Process for Ten Innovations

	Year of First Conception	Year of First Realization	Duration (Years)
Heart Pacemaker	1928	1960	32
Hybrid Corn	1908	1933	25
Hybrid Small Grains	1937	1955	19
Green Revolution Wheat	1950	1966	16
Electrophotography	1937	1959	22
Input-Output Economic Analysis	1936	1964	28
Organophosphorus Insecticides	1934	1947	13
Oral Contraceptive	1951	1960	9
Magnetic Ferrites	1933	1955	22
Video Tape Recorder	1950	1956	6
Average Duration			19.2

Obviously, only the fanatic and the irrational would have done so![8]

Return on investment, so often used as a measure of success by astute management, is also a yardstick that discourages innovation and any outlay for an R & D program. Consider, for example, what happens if such a program requires significant new plant and equipment. Current profits measured as a percentage of investment decrease because the total investment increases without a corresponding immediate return. Yet at the same time managers are under pressure to sustain and increase the percentage return. Bonuses, profit sharing, and other benefits are likely to be lower or curtailed while the managers wait for the new investment to pay off. In short, the rewards for successful programs just are not worth the penalties if an adequate immediate return is not forthcoming.

Management suffers from additional built-in constraints that inhibit it from thinking R & D. Not only do managers balk at

8. Robert D. Dean, Jr., "The Temporal Mismatch-Innovation's Pace vs. Management's Time Horizon," *Research Management,* May 1974, pp. 12 ff.

risky new concepts, but so do engineers, unions, and the sales force.[9]

Since by its very nature R & D is hazardous, professional management that spends money on it will more than likely want to direct it. But direction means control, and control, by definition, tends to thwart the very creativity that produces innovation, which in turn produces the profits that will justify the expenditure. Sophisticated management hurts creativity by tending to allocate funds to predetermined areas of research. However, the most rewarding yields are often the side paths that turn up as new knowledge is gained, the potentials in products and processes that were not foreseen when an R & D program was approved, and for the pursuit of which adequate moneys were not set aside.

Managers with established products and markets to protect are likely to resist the diversion of dollars from research intended to preserve and strengthen their existing lines. They will oppose the switching of funds to the development of untried secondary curiosities that if fruitful may well result in downgrading their own roles in the organization.

Professional administration discourages creativity even aside from a predilection not to pursue the unforeseen. Management tends all too often to distribute funds for R & D on the basis of the current status rather than of the future potential. Budgeteers tend also to take into account the pet projects of those who are in a position to influence funding. These projects soak up dollars that otherwise might be deliberately set aside for pursuing side paths uncovered in the laboratory.

Major breakthroughs are likely to come from risk acceptance, not from failure avoidance. Yet "good" management shapes organizational efforts by its desire to avoid failure rather than by a willingness to accept risk.

A few years ago, Arthur D. Little, in cooperation with the

---

9. See chapter 1, discussion of new products.

Industrial Research Institute for the National Science Foundation, made a study, "Barriers to Innovation in Industry." It indicated that the high risk of being blamed for failure was one of the most severe of 131 barrier factors studied.[10]

In the light of the foregoing, how can we expect management to advance those new ideas or concepts that could turn out eventually to be the most profitable?

The University of Sussex in Brighton, England, made a comparison of ten variables in twenty-nine pairs of innovations in the chemical and instrumentation industries. Both innovations of a pair went to the same market. One was successful, the other not. The results indicated that the use of sophisticated management techniques did not distinguish between successes and failures.[11]

Government action has been blamed for discouraging R & D in the United States. This is reflected in the results of a survey reported in *Business Week,* July 3, 1978. Surveyed companies were required to spend considerable sums on research devoted to OSHA, pollution, food and drug, and other federal requirements. This meant fewer dollars were available for technology intended to increase productivity and health. To aggravate the problem, innovation has been hampered in the large-spending chemical and drug industries by the cost and time required to satisfy government regulations for the approval of new chemicals and drugs. As a result, fewer new products are attempted, and those that are undertaken are mostly items that have large, assured markets.

10. A. D. Little and Industrial Research Institute Report to National Science Foundation, "Barriers to Innovation in Industry—Opportunities for Public Policy Changes" (NSF–C748 and C725) August 1973; as referred to by Donald M. Collier in "Research Based Venture Companies—The Link between Market and Technology," *Research Management,* May 1974, pp. 16–20.
11. "Success and Failure in Industrial Innovation," Report on Project Sappho by Science Policy Research Unit, University of Sussex, February 1972, as referred to in Collier, "Research Based Venture Companies." (See footnote 10.)

Federal regulations play a further role. For example, moneys provided by EPA for municipal waste-water treatment require that specifications be written so that equipment can be purchased from more than one source. This is as it should be, except that this rules out innovative and more efficient technology that has been developed uniquely by only one company.

Government antitrust policy may occasionally hurt in cases where superior technology derived from the laboratory is the basis of a company's dominance in an industry.

Government policy on capital gains taxation and its failure to provide fast write-offs for high-risk investments has also discouraged the development of the new. Thus, much money is needed to manufacture and market what R & D produces. The overall investment climate, therefore, is important.

The accounting profession has not helped. The 1974 ruling of the Accounting Standards Board requires expensing R & D. This means that all funds spent in one year are charged to profits in that same year. They cannot be capitalized as an investment and written off over several years as was formerly permitted.[12]

Despite all, attitudes and environment may be the major barriers to R & D. Thus, one finds many firms that spend heavily on R & D clustered around Palo Alto and Boston, which foster a special outlook and setting conducive to research and development. On the other hand, comparatively few firms spending much on R & D are found, for example around Philadelphia or Kansas City, which seemingly lack that unique atmosphere.[13]

Contrary to what some might expect, there is evidence that R & D is more efficient in small companies than in large ones. Proof is difficult. Some limited investigation, however, points in this direction. It is also interesting to point out that small companies are more productive innovators than large ones. Polaroid, Texas Instruments, and Xerox were all small

---

12. *Business Week*, July 3, 1978, p. 52.

when they started. According to one study, more than half of sixty-one important innovations of the Twentieth century have come from independent inventors or small firms. Another study has reported that two-thirds of the important innovations between 1946 and 1955 came from the same source.[13,14]

The large organization's forte is the massive development project that requires a major effort and expenditure.

If the reader accepts the premises above, could one then postulate that it would be better for large organizations to scatter their research and development efforts among small and independent groups? There might be some duplication of work, but in the long run the arrangement might be more productive than to opt for the large, centralized laboratories. Duplication is to some degree another word for competition, and our system has been built on competition.

The United States may be spending more than other countries on research and development However, the U.S. investment is concentrated in space, defense, and nuclear areas. In other countries research and development is focused on civilian programs. Table 19.2 shows comparative data for 1971, for which year information is available.

Table 19.2
Research and Development Expenditures, 1971

Country	R & D Expenditures as Percent of GNP
United States	2.6*
United Kingdom	2.1
Germany	2.0
Japan	1.8
France	1.8
Canada	1.2
Italy	.9

SOURCE: U.S. Department of Labor, as reported by James E. Seitz in "Patterns and Perspectives," *Financial Executive*, April 1977, p. 28.

*The figures reflect a downward trend, 2.73% for 1962 and 2.24% for 1978 (*U.S. News & World Report*, November 27, 1978, p. 61).

---

13. See Collier, "Research Based Venture Companies."
14. R. Charpie, "Technological Innovation, Its Environment and Management" (U.S. Department of Commerce, January 1967).

Hypotheses:

R & D pays off for an industry as well as for the nation as a whole, but not, in mature industries, for an individual firm.

The productivity of R & D is inversely proportional to the amount of control exercised by top management.

The more sophisticated a management, the less it will spend on R & D.

20

Ethical Conduct Takes Precedence Over Expediency

Reality: That supposition is all too often honored in the breach. There are literally hundreds of examples of the priority given to the expedient; or in other words, ethical considerations be damned. Philosophically, the expedient approach may have its immediate rewards, but it is immoral, and in the long run it is probably self-defeating.

It may be more advantageous in the near term to design an automobile gas tank that will cut costs, even though it gives cars an increased chance of catching fire in a rear-end collision, than to produce a design that costs more. A brand of tire doesn't hold up and may be the cause of numerous accidents. It may at the moment seem expedient to deny allegations of such a tire's fallibility, but eventually excessive publicity and government pressure will force a recall anyway. The denials merely accentuate the public's perception of corporate guilt. Although it may be wrong and in fact illegal, how often have too many people crowded into a restaurant or nightclub that has too few exits. It is expedient to let them do so, for it means extra income—at least until a fire breaks out and scores of people perish.

These are examples of people being maimed and killed as a result of deliberate decisions by top management who knew or at least should have known of the consequences.

An apparently less fatal example could involve a mixup of a toxic fire-retardant chemical and an animal feed supplement. A plant foreman through carelessness has the chemical dumped into the animal feed. Only after the contaminated feed is shipped does he belatedly discover the mistake. Does he immediately report the mishap to management, which in turn recalls the shipment, or does he hope that the amount of contaminant ingested by the cattle will harm neither the animals nor eventually the people who buy the meat. It's hard to say. In any event, the foreman will be torn between advising management and risking the axe, or taking the more expedient approach. If at a later date trouble arises, he can always deny knowledge of the matter. The art of stonewalling is not singular to the political arena. Such an example is not purely hypothetical. There have been a couple of cases concerning contaminated animal feed shipped with resulting extensive injury and litigation.

The priority of expediency in situations less immediately threatening to life and health is pervasive. Not only top managers, but all management echelons and those who are not managers, are involved. The problem of ethical conduct, however that be defined, is probably one of the most bothersome elements in business and management today.

A supplier is persuaded by its principal customer to expand a plant to care for the client's additional and anticipated requirements. Tempted by the forecast of extra profits, the supplier proceeds with the expansion but does not obtain a firm order contract from the client for the additional volume generated by the expansion. Sometime later another vendor offers the customer the same product at an unusually low price. What should the latter do? Should he now do business with the original supplier, knowing full well that if he doesn't the adverse effect on the vendor's cash flow will be drastic? It would certainly be expedient to purchase from the new vendor, but what is ethical, what is morally right, and from whose standpoint?

More examples abound. An oil company purchasing agent finds it expedient to purchase oil drums from a newly formed company owned in part by the chairman of the board, who of course has carefully avoided suggesting such a possibility.

Conventioneers get together over drinks; they talk business. It may be unlawful to fix prices, but if they're not stabilized all hell will break loose. Therefore, it is expedient to be slightly illegal.

A child needs pencils for school. It is expedient, but dishonest, to pick up a dozen at the office. The company will never miss them.

A president moves a company's headquarters from Chicago to Phoenix or San Jose to Chicago. Such a move may be tough for some of the personnel who thus find their lives and their children's lives dislocated, but whether for personal or other reasons it is expedient in the view of the decision makers.

Turning to the philosophical, why does "what's expedient" take precedence over "what's right"? To some degree the situation arises from human self-interest. Coupled with this is the fact that the preeminence of profit has been the traditional standard by which business is conducted. An enterprise has been expected to make decisions on the basis of which of various alternatives will contribute most to profits. Other considerations in the past were supposed to be of lesser importance.

In today's terms this should be broadened somewhat. Decisions are based on profit, but not solely on that criterion. They are also based on what will be best for long-run survival, effectiveness, and growth of the organization. Of course, top management's own survival, and the fulfillment of its own needs whatever they may be, are also important. The latter may on occasion give rise to conflict-of-interest and ethical problems.

There also has been increasing recognition, if but slowly,

by management that it is responsible, not alone to the organization and to the stockholders, but also to the consumer, the local community, the public at large, government, its employees, and suppliers. With responsibility comes ·a certain moral requirement for fair dealing. What constitutes fair dealing can be confused at times by the conflicting interests of the various groups to whom fairness is owed.

Let us turn to some problems posed by the question of fair dealing. It is not only unethical but also illegal to mislabel a product as to weight, content, or quality—and yet it happens. It is quite possible that certain drugs could be mislabeled and shipped through error. Suppose that any person taking the mislabeled drug could become seriously ill or even die. If management discovered the error, obviously morality would require that the drug be recalled immediately and full publicity given to protect the public. And this is without regard to any action that might be required by the government.

However, suppose the mislabeling of the drug would not cause persons taking the product any serious discomfort. What then? A costly recall would undoubtedly hurt sales volume and the company. The resultant damage and screaming publicity might have a permanent adverse effect on the company. On the other hand, if silence were kept the public would never know of the stupid but not very harmful error. What is the right thing to do, for the stockholders, for the public? What is likely to be done?

Examples of unintentional mislabeling are too numerous to set forth, but a typical error could involve a minor failure of packaging machinery resulting in a correctly identified packaged product leaving a plant underweight. In this particular instance, the error might have been discovered reasonably quickly, but not before some shipments were on the way to the consumer. The poor consumer who bought the item would have been short-changed, but without a scale he would probably remain totally unaware of any underweight.

Would the workman or foreman who discovered the mistake
and who rectified the packaging machinery go rushing off to
management to report the incident? Hardly likely, for first of
all the individual by doing so might jeopardize his job, and
secondly, recovering the specific underweight packages would
be time consuming and practically impossible. Assume no
government inspectors found out, no purchasing agents for
chains were aware of the error, and no customers complained.
All purely hypothetical but quite possible. So what happens?
Nothing! What about the matter of expediency and fairness?
What about the ethical considerations?

A manager may hear of an opening with another company
for which his young assistant would be qualified. The job
would mean a considerable increase in salary and enlarged
responsibilities. The assistant is loyal, hard working, capable,
and useful, and obviously a person difficult to replace. In fact,
any replacement would require six months' training, during
which time the manager's very own efficiency might suffer.
Does the manager morally owe it to his assistant to advise him
of the opening? To whom is the manager responsible—to his
subordinate? Yet, if he informs his assistant, is he being fair
to his company, which loses a good man for whose training
the company has paid?

Suppose a manager hears of an opening in another department in the same firm? If his assistant has not already learned
of it, should he mention the opportunity? Morally, there is no
justification to hesitate, but for some managers, expediency
may prevail.

When appraisal time comes around, how should a manager
evaluate his meritorious assistant? The process is dichotomous
—rate a person with complete honesty, and another job in the
company will be his, in which case the manager loses his
assistant. Here again, the question is even less ambiguous: To
be fair or expedient?

Examples of conflicting ethical considerations abound in

municipalities and state and federal government. Witness the GSA.

The following touch on other situations where conflicting moral perceptions exist.

Does one shut down a chemical plant or a mine in which the work is hazardous to health and life itself, but that represents the principal employment available in a community?

Does one fire an old-time, incapable but loyal employee who should never have been hired or should have been fired years ago, when he was still young enough to find another job for which he might have been competent, or keep him, at stockholder and company expense?

Is it morally right to create obsolescense, by promoting changes in fashion or by designing a product not to last long? Doing so could represent unnecessary cost to the consumer, but work to employees, growth for the company, and return on investment to stockholders.

Does a manager spend money for a lavish headquarters building and grounds to provide a pleasant place to work for employees, or to improve efficiency by putting scattered employees all under one roof, or is a new building merely a tribute to the manager's own ego? The building may be an expensive one for the stockholders.

One can hardly speak of ethical standards without a brief review of potential conflicts between interests of management and those of the enterprise, its stockholders, employees, colleagues, and vendors. Do any of the following items raise questions as to possible conflicts of interest?

- Receiving personal favors in respect to mortgages, other loans, purchases, services, and investment opportunities from banks and vendors doing business with the enterprise. This is less flagrant than direct bribery and kickbacks.
- Stretching to the limit the fringe benefit called "expense account."
- Management grossly overpaying itself.

- Empire building where it serves a manager's ego but is only an expense for the enterprise.
- Hiring and promoting relatives in lieu of other, more capable prospective and current employees.
- Similarly granting franchises to relatives or other favorites in lieu of more capable prospective franchisees.
- Generally, for personal and selfish reasons, and not alone where a sexual liaison is involved, playing favorites with employees as to overtime pay, promotions, layoffs, and assignments to desirable or undesirable jobs.
- Selectively communicating information about others, by a manager, to make himself look good.
- Stealing or withholding credit for suggestions.

The following, too, raise questions concerning ethics.

- Covering up poor performance or quality defects.
- More generally, providing misleading information, omitting pertinent information, actually falsifying information —for financial statements, in internal reports, on data relating to efficiency and quality of product, in figures submitted to government agencies, etc.
- Unfair persecution of a capable employee until he is driven to quit.
- Age discrimination in hiring, partly to save pension-related costs.
- Discrimination because of race, sex, or other biases.
- Laying off competent people and keeping on the incompetent because of seniority.
- Pressuring dealers and customers to buy Product Y if they want Product X, when X is in short supply and Y is not.
- Providing misleading price information to prospective customers.
- Selling a product believed by some to be harmful—for example, sugar cereals for children.
- Taking advantage of inside financial information.

We've already touched on it, but again, why do individuals who believe themselves equally as ethical as their neighbors, and on a personal basis are, allow themselves to operate with different standards in business, or for that matter, in nonbusiness enterprises?

There is a tendency to separate personal from organization ethics. Loyalty to the enterprise has a high priority. To some degree this is the heritage of a profit ethos influenced by the early history of the industrial revolution and the harsh realities encountered in developing the resources of a continent.

There are pressures for both survival and for promotion within an organization. Even the man who has already reached the top is under continual pressure to retain that position. In general, managers have a strong competitive spirit and tend to place high priority on the importance of winning. This psyche, and a certain amount of selfishness entwined with it, are two of the characteristics that enable an individual to work his way through the managerial ranks on up to the higher levels.

In the effort to progress upward, how far does one go in bending or breaking the rules of good ethical conduct? Loyalty to the company and its objectives is an asset. Loyalty means that other things are secondary. With time, do the competitive spirit, the high priority on winning, loyalty to the enterprise, and personal selfishness mesh, reinforce each other, and become ever more deeply ingrained as part of the individual's psyche?

How really widespread is the pressure on managers to compromise personal morality for company goals? Pitney-Bowes, Incorporated, surveyed its managers anonymously, and in January, 1977, published the results. So did Uniroyal, Incorporated in 1976. Fully 59 percent of Pitney-Bowes managers surveyed and 70 percent of Uniroyal's admitted to feeling pressured to compromise personal ethics to achieve company goals—which likely means the managers feel that compromise is important to their upward progression. Most managers, for both companies, would not refuse orders to market off-standard and possibly dangerous items. The surveys indicated that in both companies well over two-thirds of young managers automatically go along with superiors in order to show their loyalty, which is important to survival and promotion in the company.[1]

That personal morality is compromised by company managers is perceived by the public. Thus the majority of respondents in a 1977 public opinion survey by Louis Harris & Associates and Marketing Science Institute, for Sentry Insurance Company, agreed with the following: "Most companies are so concerned about profit they don't care about quality." "Most manufacturers don't really care about giving consumers a fair deal." Almost half of the respondents thought warranties were written "mainly for the protection of manufacturers." Fully 78 percent believed that products "don't last as long as they used to." Half believed the consumer today is "getting a worse deal in the marketplace" than he got ten years before.[2]

Managers who feel pressured to compromise personal ethics for the sake of company loyalty can rationalize the separation of business from personal morality in a number of ways.

Loyalty to the company is akin to the loyalty afforded his client by an attorney, or so it could be argued. The company is the manager's client.

One of the most common defenses against charges of immoral behavior has always been the claim that one was acting under orders.

Another rationale is, The other fellow does it, and I have to compete with him; and still another, The rules are unfair; they help the other guy and hinder me; my circumstances are different. Then there is always the argument that one is only redressing past wrongs, or injustices or unfair tactics.

The ethics of business represent the ethics of society, or perhaps the ethics that society is willing to accept. Only when society widely insists on higher standards will management feel impelled to implement them. Management feels more

---

1. "The Pressure to Compromise Personal Ethics," *Business Week*, January 31, 1977, p. 107.
2. As reported by James J. Kilpatrick in "A Conservative View," *San Jose Mercury*, June 3, 1977.

comfortable following society's rules. In part perhaps, acceptance of higher standards will be hastened by the threat of government action. Such action may actually be welcomed where it forces acceptance by everyone of that which is right, not merely expedient.

The incursion by government in setting ethical standards, as with antidiscrimination regulations, may also at times expedite a general acceptance of higher standards. Even forced acceptance, after a period of implementation in practice, tends to be rationalized into willing acceptance. It becomes customary, and part of the rules of the game.

Society's and also management's expectations and standards of morality are higher today than in the past. Both groups are more sensitive to and less tolerant of unethical behavior, so that at this juncture in the evolution of our business philosophy there is an increasing awareness of conduct that fails to conform to good ethical practice.

Hypothesis:

Expediency tends to override what's right. This tendency is proportional to the amount of utility derived from expediency and inversely proportional to the amount of disutility. Utility refers to the extra rewards incurred, or penalties avoided, from action based on expediency. Disutility refers to the amount of discomfort that results from not doing what's right, and that in turn depends on the strength of the individual's ethical conviction and the pressure generated by society's accepted mores.

Index

Ability, and promotion, 79
Accident rate, 104
Acquired tastes, and compulsion,
    103
Acquisitions, and growth, 156
Administrator. *See* Manager
Advertising, 104
Age discrimination suits, 117
Allocated funds, spending of,
    143–44
American Management
    Association, 118
Appraisal, formal, conclusions
    regarding, 120–21;
    consistency of, 118, 119;
    danger of, 120; difficulties
    of, 115–17; discrimitory
    nature of, 118; distortion
    of, 115–17; halo effect in,
    115, 116, 117; honesty of,
    115–16; method of, 119–20;
    negative aspect of, 115;

negative aspects of, 115;
    nuisance of, 120;
    objectivity of, 118; and
    personal traits, 118; positive
    aspects of, 115; purpose of,
    117; raises and, 116;
    subjectivity of, 118;
    validity of, 119; variability
    of, 120
Areas of research, 161
Authority, delegation of, 55–56;
    and factors of
    centralization, 73
Authority and responsibility,
    delegation of, 57–58;
    separation of, 56–57
Autonomy, 73; and computer
    capacity, 74; and staff size,
    74

Belief, and planning, 134

Big business, 1; and managerial
    control, 19
Blue collar workers, 93, 109;
    and desire for security,
    111, 112
Board of directors, 77
Bosses, multiple, 52
Budget, as compromise, 140–41;
    deemphasized, 144;
    cost-cutting tool, 144;
    detail in, 149; and
    disharmony, 145–46; fixed,
    147, 148; and game playing,
    142; manipulation of,
    140–41; operating, 139;
    problems of, 140–41;
    purpose of, 139–40; and
    status quo, 143; usefulness
    of, 146–47; variable,
    147–48; and waste, 143
Bureaucracy, 79, 132, 153; and
    top management, 79
Business, and research and
    development spending, 158
Business, large, advantages of,
    41, 42; and governmental
    encouragement, 44; and
    efficiency, 43; profits, 43
Business, small, advantages of,
    41–42; problems of, 42
Business ethics, and societal
    control, 175
Business philosophy, and ethical
    standards, 176
Businessman, as entrepreneur, 1

Capital, and loss of
    entrepreneurial control, 5;
    and prudent man rule, 15
Cash-flow, 12
Centralization, 75
Change, 149
Challenge, 106, 113; rejection
    of, 111–12
Circumstance, and business
    growth, 21–22; and profits,
    25

Comfort level, 73; and
    departmental autonomy,
    73, 74
Communication, bypass, 59, 60;
    morale and, 61; movement
    of, 59–60; organizational,
    59–62; problems of, 62
Computer, 44; capacity and
    managerial control, 74
Conflict, and objectives, 128–29
Conformity, 87
Competition, 158, 175
Competitive spirit, 174
Conflict of interest, 169, 172–73
Conformity, of management, 15
Contentment. See Happiness
Controlled aggressiveness, and
    business growth, 16–17;
    and personal performance,
    17–18
Controller, 146
Cost cutting, and budget, 144
Cost estimates, 147–48
Creative research, 98
Creativity, and job happiness,
    104
Cultural background, 109

Decentralization, 146
Decision making, 135
Delegate, ability to, 62
Delegation of responsibility,
    47–49, 50
Demotivating jobs, 104
Directorships, interrelationship
    of, 78
Discontent, fostered, 103
Disutility, 176
Double standard, 82–83
Duties, definition of, 65

Effectiveness, decline of, 166
Egnaro. See Orange Shirt
    Principle
Eitzen, D. Stanley, 166
Electronics industry, research
    and development in, 156

Electrostatic copying, 13
Entrepreneur, 1; and growth, 5; as business founder, 3; and business takeover, 4–5; defined, 2; negative management potential of, 5–6
Error rate, 104
Ethical conduct, 167, 168
Ethical considerations, 172–73; and business, 174; conflicting, 171–72; personal, 174
Ethical questions, 173
Ethical standards, and government, 176
Expectations, and objectives, 107; and performance, 107–108; role of, 108
Expediency, 176; examples of, 167–69; and human self-interest, 169; priority of, 168–69

Fair dealing, problems of, 170, 171
Fixed budget. *See* Budget
Fixed cost, 151
Ford, Henry, as entrepreneur-manager, 2
Ford Motor Company, 118
Forecast, 138, 147; and planning, 133, 134
Free enterprise system, 1

G & A. *See* Overhead
Game-playing, and budget, 142–43
Games, 131
Gambler, 2
General and administrative expense. *See* Overhead
Goals, clash of, 85; organizational, 85; personal, 85;
Good management, principles of, 45

Government, research and development and, 157
Graham, Bill, 3
Growth, 43, 126

Halo effect, 115, 116
Happiness, 109; and job pressures, 103; and job turnover, 104; and productivity, 101, 103
High risk expenditure, 155
History, and planning, 134
Horizontal job rotation, 106–107
Hull, Raymond, 5
Human self-interest, 169
Hypothesis, 19–20, 25, 39, 44, 53–54, 63, 72, 75, 83, 87–88, 99, 109, 113, 120–21, 132, 138, 148–49, 153, 165, 176

Ideas, and problem solving, 93
Implementation, 71
Indifference, job related, 105
Individual, essential to organization, 87
Industrial research funds, allocation of, 157
Inflation, 116
Initiative, and job happiness, 104
Innovation, barriers to, 162–63; and financing, 11; and market distribution, 10–11; opposition to, 113; and risk taking, 9–10; and small companies, 13–14; source of, 164; and steel industry, 157; threat to management, 11–12; time lapse and, 159–60; and timing, 9–10
Insecurity, 109; and protection, 101

Job, attitudes toward, 96; means to end, 103–105
Job dissatisfaction poll, 105
Job enlargement. *See* Job enrichment

Job enrichment, 108, 109
Job hopper, 82
Job rotation, 106
Job satisfaction, decline in, 105;
    survey of, 105
Job security, and productivity,
    101

Kicking upstairs, 68–69
Knowledge, and problem
    solving, 92

Leadership, and circumstances,
    98
Line, functions, 49, 50; relation
    to staff, 50–51
Line managers, 50
Line-staff relationships,
    dilemmas of, 55–56
Logicality, and budget, 148–49
Loyalty, 174–75

MBO. *See* Management by
    objective
Management, aggressiveness of,
    137; as guide, 137;
    autocratic, 90–93; and
    board of directors, 77, 78;
    and budget, 144–45,
    146–48; bureaucracy, 79;
    caretaker role of, 21;
    comfort level of, 73;
    conflict of interests,
    172–73; controls by, 33;
    and creativity, 161;
    dilemmas of, 27–29; and
    double standard, 82; and
    expedience, 168; fair
    dealing by, 171; hierarchy
    of, 80; horizontal structure
    of, 48, 49; importance of,
    137–38; and levels of
    performance, 33;
    limitations of, 21–22,
    24–25; manipulative
    techniques of, 38–39;
    orange shirt principle,

91–92; and overhead,
    152–53; personal objective
    of, 29–33; personality and
    objectives, 126; and
    planning, 136; practice and
    theory, 46–53; primary
    goals of, 27; principal
    objectives of, 39; priorities
    of, 27–29; and problems of
    company growth, 5–6; and
    profit control, 35–38; and
    proxies, 77–78; and
    research and development,
    158–59, 160–61;
    responsibility of, 170;
    societal ethics of, 176;
    styles, 97; and vagueness,
    65; variations of, 98–99;
    vertical structure, 48; X
    type, 98; Y type, 98
Management, participative,
    90–93, 94; limitations of,
    94
Management by objectives, 119;
    and conflicts, 128–29;
    confusion of, 124; dangers
    of, 128; defined, 123;
    effectiveness of, 132; game
    playing by, 131; managerial
    appraisal of, 130–31;
    personal element in,
    126–27; real objective, 124;
    results of, 129; and
    specifics, 127–28; spelling
    out details in, 125;
    subjectivity of, 126;
    vagueness of, 125;
    variability of, 126–27;
    workability, 131
Manager, ability of, 24, 25; as
    administrator, 1; and
    appraisal, 116, 117; and
    budget presure, 144–45;
    and challenge, 106; and
    comfort level, 73, 74;
    competition of, 174;
    concerns of, 13; and cost

control, 148; defined, 2; ethics of, 174; in matrix management, 71; and job dissatisfaction, 105–106; and management by objective, 130; non-owner, 4; objectives of, 126; personal goals of, 85, 87; personal philosophy of, 98; and pressures, 174; and prudent man rule, 14, 15; rationalization by, 175; relationship with subordinates, 46; risk-taking attitudes, 7–8; and security, 112; threatened, 118; X-type, 95–97; Y-type, 90, 91, 92, 93, 94
Market, 43
Market distribution, 10–11
Matrix management, 70–71, 72
Measurements, departmental, 86
Mislabeling, 170–71
Monotony, susceptibility to, 109
Morality, separation of personal and business, 174–75
Motivation, 129–30

Negotiating process, and budget, 142
Nepotism, 81
Nonconformity, 87
Nonperformance, and profits, 31

Objectives, personal, 130
Obsolescence, 11
Office space, 75
Opinion, and planning, 136
Opinion Research Corporation, 105
Opposing interests, measurement of minimization, 86; minimization of, 85–86
Operating budget. *See* Budget
Orange Shirt Principle, 91–92
Orders, 175

Organization, size, 80; size related to vagueness, 69
Organization charts, 66; dangers of, 69–70
Organizational disharmony, and budget, 145–46
Organizational unit, autonomy of, 73
Organizations, areas of authority in, 67, 69; structural vagueness of, 67–68
Overhead, related to sales volume, 151; tradition of, 153; variable costs of, 151; volume of business and, 151
Overspending, 143–44
Overtime, 107–108

Pacemaker, 12
Packard, David, as entrepreneur-manager, 2
Parkinson's Law, 43, 153
Participation, drawbacks of, 96
Participatory decision making, 93–94
Passive resistance, 103, 109
People, and adaptation to jobs, 96
Perceived insecurity, 103, 104
Performance, 31–33, 77, 86, 109, and budget, 146; and expectation and desires, 129; and job satisfaction, 108–109; and management, 25; measurement of, 119; and profits, 32
Personal morality, pressure to compromise, 174–75
Personal satisfaction, 30
Peter, Lawrence J., 5
Peter Principle, The 4–5
Planning, conservative outlook in, 136; defined, 133; deviations from, 137; elements beyond managerial control, 133–34; factors

Planning (*continued*)
  involved in, 133–34;
  flexibility of, 136; influence
  on forecast, 134–35;
  internal factors in, 134;
  luck in, 136; optimistic
  outlook in, 136–37;
  rationality in, 135;
  subjective expecattions of,
  134
Polaroid, 14, 163
Pressure, and job happiness, 103
Productivity, 101, 103, 104
Profit quotas, 108
Profits, 31, 32, 126, 152, 153,
  174; and autonomy of
  organizational unit, 73;
  and expediency, 169;
  increase of, 37–38; and
  management, 25;
  manipulation of, 39;
  reduction of, 35–37;
  validity of, 34–35;
  variability of, 34–35
Promotion, 80, 81–82; potential
  for, 119; and pressures, 174
Proxies, 77–78
Prudent man rule, 14, and
  investment and conformity,
  14–15
Public opinion, of company
  ethics, 175

Quality of output, 104
R & D. *See* Research and
  development
Raise, 116
Rationality, 135, 138; and
  budgets, 140
Research and development, 93;
  barriers to, 162–63; and
  business spending, 158; and
  businesses, 157; cost of,
  158; and creativity, 161;
  discouragement of,
  158–59; expenditure by
  country, 164; and

government spending, 157;
  in country as whole, 155;
  and industrial research
  funds, 157; and investment
  returns, 160; investment
  risk in, 155; and private
  industry, 156; and small
  companies, 163; time span
  involved, 158
Resistance, 103
Responsibility, delegation of,
  55–56
Retirement, 106
Rigidity, 69
Risk, avoidance of, 158–59, 161,
  162; managerial
  minimization of, 2
Risk taking, 1, 6; controlled,
  7–8; failure potential in, 8;
  growth, 6; and investments,
  11; managerial avoidance
  of, 12–19; and managerial
  performance, 7–8; and
  market distribution, 10–11;
  premature, 9–10; problems
  of avoidance, 18; and
  prudent man rule, 14; and
  small businessman, 6; and
  timing, 9–10
Rockefeller, John D., as
  entrepreneur-manager, 2
Routine, controllable, 112;
  preference for, 111–12
Rules, flexibility of, 62

Sales campaign, participation
  in, 93
Sales quotas, 108
Sales volume, 152, 153
School tie, 81
Security, 109, 111; and job type,
  104; and production, 101
Seniority, 101
"Skip-level" meetings, 61
Slightly illegal, 169
Small business, research and
  development in, 163, 164

Span of control, 45, 46
Spending, high and low risk, 158
Staff, 52; function, 49, 50; size
    and managerial control of,
    74
Status quo, and budget, 149
Steel industry, innovations in,
    157; research and
    development in, 157
Stockholders, 32
Structure, organizational. *See*
    Organization chart
Subordinates, bypassing of,
    58–59; and Y-type
    manager, 91
Superfluity, 94
Survival, 27, 29–30, 126, 169,
    174; as managerial
    objective, 27, 28–30;
    managerial need for, 8–9
Synergism, 6
System, violation of, 62, 63

Technology, 41, 42
Terkel, Studs, 96
Texas Instruments, 13, 163
Theory X management, 89, 90,
    91, 92, 93; and
    unstimulating jobs, 89;
    implications of, 90
Theory Y management, 89, 90,
    91, 92, 93, 94, 95; people
    oriented, 90
Time lapse. *See* Innovations
Timing, 9–10, 98; and
    promotion, 80
Tradition, 158
Transistors, 13
Trustee, conformity of, 14;

discrimination by, 14–15;
    investment by, 14
Turnover, 104, 106

Unhappiness, 109; and
    production, 101
Underspending, 146
United States, industrial
    companies, 79; research and
    development program, 164
University of Sussex, 162
Utility, 176

Vagueness, 65; in organizational
    authority, 68–69, 137; and
    matrix management, 70–71
Value systems, 109
Variable budget. *See* Budget
Variable cost, 151, 153
Vertical job rotation, 107
Volkswagen, 11

Wall Street Journal, The, 78, 79
Waste, and budget, 142–43
White collar workers, 109
Who-you-know, 81
Working, 96

Xerox, 13, 163
X-type manager, and
    advancement, 97;
    advantages of, 95; cost
    cutting and, 96

Yetman, N. R., 106
Y-type manager, confusion with
    X-type, 90–91; democratic,
    90; participative, 89;
    disadvantages of, 95